Praise for
Emotional Science

"The training is highly valuable. Afterward it all seemed obvious, but the process was insightful and liberating. I realized I was creating the issue."
—S. KINSEY, *General Manager Agile, SAI Global*

"The takeaway for me…was understanding how overreactions to events or circumstances are rooted in past emotional scars and can be acknowledged and explored. Powerful stuff!"
—G. BECK, *Agile Practice Area Director at Plaster Group, LLC*

"Forget all you've heard… Be prepared to meet the unexpected within yourself."
—E. AYBERK, *Managing Partner, Fifty1*

"This model is extremely helpful as I strive to find constructive ways to deal with my emotions. As an Agile coach, I strive every day to manage my emotions so that I can better serve others on their journey. By using this model, I have a deliberate method of processing the myriad emotions that surface while I face challenges with my environment and with other people."
—J. SCHREUDER, *Director, Agile Program Office at ARCA Worldwide*

"Both Michael and Audree have the emotional beast by its horns. They guide you to emerge out of the emotional trap."
—G. SALWAN, *Scrum Master, AIMIA Inc.*

"Simplified a deep topic to something with practical applicability whilst remaining insightful, honest, and true."
—R. Bunning Principal Trainer (CST) and Agile Coach, *Scrum With Style*

"*Emotional Science* made easy and it really works!"
—M. Poonawala, *Agile Project Manager, sHub ScotiaBank*

"Fantastic exercises and highly revealing."
—S. Mitchell Sr. Agile Coach, *Commonwealth Bank of Australia*

"I gained a deeper understanding of how my past has been controlling my present and how to regain control to flip the script on my life."
—M. Tielemans, *Founder, Meraki Marketing*

Emotional Science

The Key to Unlocking High Performance

Emotional Science

The Key to Unlocking High Performance

Audree Tara and Michael K Sahota

Copyright © 2018 by Audree Tara and Michael K Sahota

All rights reserved.

Editing and Book Development Provided By
The Awakened Press
www.theawakenedpress.com

Cover and Interior Design by David Moratto
Mandala (✤) by Shari Schubot

No part of this publication may be reproduced, stored in a retrieval system, or transmitted in any form or by any means, electronic, mechanical, recording or otherwise, without the prior written permission of the authors, except by a reviewer who wishes to quote brief passages in connection with a review written for inclusion in a print or online medium, magazine, newspaper, periodical, or broadcast.

This publication provides content related to educational, medical, and psychological topics; however, it is not intended to be a substitute for the medical advice of a licensed physician. The authors are not licensed as medical professionals, psychologists, or psychiatrists, and the reader should consult with their doctor on any matters relating to his/her health. All matters regarding health require medical supervision. Further, understand that the guidance contained herein is not intended as a substitute for consultation with a licensed medical, educational, or health care professional and usage of the material implies the acceptance of this disclaimer. Before beginning any change in lifestyle in any way, it is recommended to consult a licensed professional to ensure that one is doing what is best for one's own situation.

The material in this publication is for personal use only, and not for commercial applications. Commercial use of this material requires licensing agreement and training with certification from the authors.
The following terms are licensed trademarks of the authors:
Emotional Science
Emotional Freedom System
Get Clear Technique

The resources provided are accurate at the time of publication.

First edition.

ISBN: 978-0-9949904-9-5

We would like to thank all our teachers in life
Our Parents: Sarwan, Irene, Roberta, Marshall, and Evelyn
Our Children: Scarlett, Clifton, Sean, Samantha, and Nate
Our Friends: for their support throughout our journey
Our Book Team: Lindsay R. Allison, Linda Phillips-Smith,
and David Moratto
Our Students, Clients, and Members of the Agile Community:
for demonstrating the effectiveness of this work
through their application

And a special thank you to:
Oneness University and O&O Academy
for supporting our growth

Contents

Word From The Editor . . . . *xiii*
Prologue — Michael . . . . *xvii*
Prologue — Audree . . . . *xxi*
Leadership And High Performance . . . . *xxv*
Who We Are . . . . *xxvii*

1   Get Ready To Experiment 1
2   Your Emotional Truth 11
3   Emotions: It's Not What You Think 19
4   Emotions 101: How Emotions Work 37
5   Working With Emotions 57
6   Emotional Freedom Checklist 63
7   Get Clear Technique 73
8   Enhanced Emotional Awareness 81
9   Advanced Topics 95
10 Continue The Journey 109

References 115
Further Reading 117

Index of Exercises

Chapter 2
Exercise: Your Emotional Understanding *12*
Exercise: Your Emotional Belief System *15*
Exercise: How Well Do You Understand How Your Emotions Work? . . *15*

Chapter 3
Exercise: Emotions Happen *21*
Exercise: Happy Memory *23*
Bonus Exercise: A Happy Future *27*
Exercise: Other People's Reactions *28*
Exercise: When Life Hits Us *31*
Emotional Reality Check *33*

Chapter 6
Checklist: Emotional Freedom *65*
    Step 1: Stop And Notice The Negative Emotion *65*
    Step 2: Observe The Physical Sensation *65*
    Step 3: Check To See If The Emotional Response Makes Sense . . *66*
    Step 4: Accept That It Is An Emotion From The Past *67*
    Step 5: Stop Trying To Change The Present *68*
    Step 6: Stop Reacting From The Emotional Wound *68*
    Step 7: Let Go Of Identification *70*
Summary: The Emotional Freedom Checklist *72*

Chapter 7
Get Clear Technique: Get Ready *74*
Get Clear Technique: Steps *74*
Get Clear Technique: 40 Day Practice *78*

Chapter 8

4 Traps Of The Mind	82
Trap #1: Looping Thoughts	83
Trap #2: Caught In A Story	85
Sub-Trap: Let Go Of The "Why"	88
Trap #3: Arguing	89
Exercise: Exploring How Arguments Feel	90
Trap #4: Complaining And Venting	91
Exercise: Exploring The Venting Trap	92

Chapter 9

Exercise: Handling Multiple Emotional Charges	97
Exercise: Accelerate Your Growth At The Movies	97
Exercise: Inner Investigation Of Emotions In Conflict	102
Exercise: Inventory Of Personality Patterns	105
Exercise: Investigation Of Conflicting Personality Parts	106

Chapter 10

Exercise: How Well Do You Understand How Your Emotions Work?	110

Word From The Editor

Growing up I almost always felt disconnected from the people around me and absent from the world. In truth, I could not fully relate to anyone at all. I was constantly wishing something to be different. There were some of what I would call "happy" moments, and some instances where I felt truly alive and awake, but those were rare and few and far in between.

In every essence of my being I believed I was living in a waking nightmare. As a young adult I was diagnosed with epilepsy and anxiety and was prescribed medication. My world became more and more closed off. I found a sense of aliveness in reading, where I was able to travel into as many worlds as I wanted to, without any limits. But my relationships with others were loose and fleeting, and I still felt disconnected and separated inside. I became closed and terrified of speaking my mind. I was so unhappy I did not even realize I was unhappy.

With numerous, incremental daily changes in lifestyle, the epilepsy and anxiety would eventually and completely cure. I was able to get off medication due to my mindset and meditation practice. I began applying more mindset and healing principles on myself. I buried myself in more books.

Throughout my life I learned dozens of healing techniques in order to remain medication-free, such as: hypnosis; NLP; various forms of therapy; spiritual teachings such as reading religious texts; energy healing; social work courses; retreats; and many other therapies — all followed through to their recommended completion. Some of these tools I still incorporate in various areas of my life. From a very early age I tested what seemed like everything I could get a hold of on myself in order to grow and improve. And although all of these options are relevant and effective in their own way, none of these strategies seemed to offer a lasting solution when it came to healing myself and improving on an ongoing basis. I knew by experience that the body has an internal mechanism for healing. But the strategies I had learned were proving inadequate. Most felt like Band-Aids losing their adhesive quickly as I kept trying to hastily paste them back down.

Shortly before I received this project a traumatic event happened to me that would change the course of my life. At the time my mind had blocked it out completely, like it was part of some sectioned off dream in someone else's life somewhere far off in the distance. I simply kept on going. Without being completely aware of it, I was denying reality. I refused to see that this event occurred and started to truly believe that it was a story I had created for myself. I felt I had come to the end of the line. One day I sat up in bed and cried. I prayed the hardest, clearest prayer I had ever prayed in my entire life. "God," I said. "I just want to understand my emotions. Please, I just need to understand my emotions. Because I think that when I understand them, I can understand myself more and find the answers I'm looking for."

Within the exact same day, I received a message from Michael K Sahota. We did not previously know one another. It was obvious that something bigger was happening so we agreed to work together. We practiced these exercises and I learned how to heal myself in new magnificent ways. Finally, I discovered that these were the tools I was subconsciously searching for. The healing came remarkably fast.

By the time we had done most of the emotional clearing work, it was sometime in May 2017. I had cleared most of the trauma away in a matter of 5 months. I was floored. I had accomplished this myself purely through these exercises on my own time. This outcome is, by no long shot, a gift.

The healing work I have done with Michael and Audree has elevated me to function at my greatest potential. It was their tools that helped me take my own blinders off and come to terms with traumatic events from the past. Previous instances were not an alternate reality I had constructed, and with that slow realization the true work began. Before I met Michael I felt I had few coping skills; I did not know how to live, I was not functioning properly and thought I was alone and had no one to turn to.

I became alive again by using the techniques that are shared in this book. With this came an acknowledgement and a deep internal acceptance of myself. My reality has turned more than 180 degrees since, and getting brighter and brighter each day. This is an understatement. In addition to professionally working on related material, I read the equivalent of four to five books per week, mostly within the nonfiction personal development sector. Michael and Audree's work is unsurpassed for practical tools for living and functioning to your highest being. I can safely say that I have never before come across anything like this.

The level of growth I receive daily from integrating this information into my life heals me to a level that no other therapist, teacher, or trainer can do. This is because it is not a teaching so much as it is an unlearning process, a reminder, and a reconnection to our own internal wisdom. We are simply reconnecting with that awakening.

In essence Michael and Audree have helped me to recognize and see my own greatness. That alone is guiding me back to life. I started off with a desire to live, and this work helped me come back to life at a rate that was previously unimaginable.

You are not alone. Our light can get brighter. The human mind and soul is not a project. Humans are not broken pieces of things to be fixed. We do not have broken souls, we just have to remember our true nature. I am still learning. Every day I learn. The more appropriate word is *unlearn*. For only when we unlearn can we find that place of inner knowing. And for me, the healing truly began with these emotional exercises.

That day I decided that I would choose to live began with a path of healing. My desire to stay alive accelerated with this book and these teachings. I can truly say that *Emotional Science* and my relationship with Michael and Audree has helped me to save my own life. I don't know what I would have done without it or them.

—Lindsay R. Allison
Founder, Editor In Chief
The Awakened Press

PROLOGUE

Michael

When I was young I didn't feel good about myself as a person. I did not feel worthwhile. And no matter what I might do or accomplish, at the core of my existence I did not feel whole.

As a young boy I learned that speed and efficiency were king. It was about the results. There was no place for emotion. Later, in school, I learned to use ego to feel good about myself as a human being. I saw I was much smarter than others and used this to prop up my self-worth. As a result, "everyone is an idiot" became a core part of my identity and my way of looking at the world. I looked down on others and felt superior to them.

Fast-forward to my working life where I left a scorched trail of damaged relationships. To make things work, I would just jump in and show other people how to do it. I could see people struggling to understand. All I really wanted to do was help, so I did. But imagine my surprise when instead of my fellow coworkers being grateful for my generous help, they were angry and frustrated.

If you are familiar with the character Dr. Sheldon Cooper on *The Big Bang Theory*, you'll know that he often struggles with patience, discretion, and empathy. He really reminds me a lot of myself—how I used to be. Everyone would see the brilliance, but they also saw the egotistical jerk. And just as I would write them off, they would also do the same with me.

The only people who were safe were the ones who matched my intelligence, or the ones who could see past my behaviors and forgive me. I recall asking a good friend of mine how long he had known about certain features of my personality. Answer: the entire time he knew me. And then he added, "But no one is perfect."

I became very aware that I totally sucked at self-kindness. I read the quote: "You can only be kind to others to the extent you can be kind to yourself."[1] While reading Brené Brown on the airplane, I started to cry. I knew my inner critic was brutal. *With such low levels of self-kindness,* I thought, *what kind of father am I? What kind of friend? What kind of team player am I?*

So I set a course for self-worth and started running experiments. I call it an "epic quest" to emulate a game metaphor. I learned this model from Jane McGonigal's gamification system for health.[2] I imagined a "self-kindness fuel gauge." The game is to run experiments to advance the needle. It started on low—maybe 5%. My goal was to get it to 100%.

On my epic quest I tried anything and everything I could think of. I read books, started a gratitude log, I began meditating, and went to personal development retreats. I channeled my energy into my growth as a human being. The years of hell acted as a painful chrysalis for personal transformation.

I am an experimental scientist: I measure results. And the results were startling and amazing. As I started doing the work, for the first time in my life I became deeply connected to myself. I learned that

---

1. Brown, Brené, *I Thought It Was Just Me: Women Reclaiming Power and Courage in a Culture of Shame* (New York: Gotham Books, A Division of Penguin Group [USA] Inc., 2007).
2. Jane McGonigal and Keith Wakeman, "Super Better," SuperBetter, LLC, 2018, www.superbetter.com.

self-worth is about valuing myself and seeing other people as human beings, as well. This is when I started to share these lessons with others.

My deep understanding is that *I have valued results more than people.* For me it was all about the drive for results. This gives incredible power and focus solely to the outcome. Unfortunately, by categorizing people as secondary to results, their feelings and emotions were also secondary and had no place in my methodology for how to interact with them.

Two years after I began my epic quest for kindness, my inner world was much cleaner. There was still a voice inside my head, but it was mostly kind to me. It told me how I did a good job. How it was okay not to be perfect. I thought I was at about 98% kind to myself and declared victory. Quest over. Or so I thought, yet it wasn't. It was a false victory, and my search continued. The book you are reading now is the result of my ongoing journey for inner peace.

Over the many years since that time, I still sometimes value results over people. I now strive for valuing results and valuing people, both at the same time. Not one over the other. It is an ongoing journey.

Emotional Science was written to share with others what I have learned—and dare I say—the *secret sauce* for my emotional well-being. It has been and continues to be a critical ingredient for my inner peace and the success that comes from it. Happy trails.

—Michael

PROLOGUE

Audree

As a child, I was different. I saw the world as a moving tapestry of color, sound, and emotion. I didn't fit into anything conventional, and it showed. I was a blonde-haired, blue-eyed child living with a family comprised of dark hair and brown eyes, yet that wasn't the reason I didn't belong. I was adopted into a family that I did not want to be a part of. To realize this truth took me 40 years of soul searching. I always thought it was their fault.

My childhood was spent rebelling against the system—any system. I was a challenging child. I behaved as if everything wrong in my life was the fault of others. All my pain and suffering was blamed on my external world: my parents, my grandparents, my sisters, and teachers. Never looking at myself, yet how could I? I was hurt at a very young age and this hurt just kept piling up as the years moved forward.

I left home at age 14, thinking I knew it all. It was easy to get wrapped up in the grind of life with no discernible skills, tools, or emotional support from family or friends. I stayed isolated and at best very surface-level in relating to people, other than to survive.

In my world it would have been easy to end up on the street. I was lucky that I had a few people along the way that saw something in me and guided me. I also had my spiritual life—a beacon that kept me from potentially dangerous situations.

As I grew older I realized that I was in deep pain and if I continued on the path I was on I would never be happy or successful. I was smart and talented, yet I seemed to make the wrong choices for my life. I developed a deep hidden anger and a strong rejection of others. I pushed away everything that was good in my life. Regrettably I was not in a position where those bad choices could be mended. I wanted a better life, and could only count on myself to make that happen.

I supported myself through post-secondary school; traditional university was the first route I took. I thought it was the right path, but it wasn't long before I became bored of it. While on my way to study medical illustration, I found my calling as a massage therapist. With this work a new world opened up: the connection between the body and the mind. This theory made sense to me. It also led me to begin to explore and develop my gifts as a healer.

As I worked in a quiet, dark room my healing gifts began to open up. I was able to read people in a way I never had before. There were also very strange things that would happen with colors, sound, and knowing. Then I had a dream that led me to discover energetic healing. So I did additional research and came across books about the human energy system and physical healing. This curiosity propelled me on a new educational path.

Little did I understand that the path of becoming a healer would require a deep exploration into my own pain and suffering. I was graded, not on my abilities as a healer (although it was important), I was also evaluated on my own awareness of my psychological state. My wounds, hidden masks, and defenses became exposed to everyone, including myself. It turns out all of my pain and suffering, all my problems and insufficiencies, including my failures or absence of the life I desired was no one's fault but my own.

Yet instead of feeling defeated, this brought me great joy and awareness. I was ready to hear the truth of how I was the one who was keeping myself from achieving my fullest potential. I learned to heal the emotional wounds that kept me from living a happy and successful life.

I spent the next 20 years becoming educated through experiencing tools and techniques that led me to where I am on my journey today. I learned much from the 12 years of formal training in both psychology and advanced energetic healing techniques. While I made mistakes during these years, I lived the teachings. To heal and transform others you must first heal and transform yourself.

I continue to travel the world studying ancient and modern techniques that shift the state of consciousness to create high-performance teams and vibrant individual health. I look carefully at my own beliefs and behaviors, to find meticulous precision in how my mind creates realities. I learned to love myself, I have mended my relationships and cleared away the hurt that caused so much pain and suffering. I no longer have a subconscious need to hurt myself or others and I can say that this journey I have been on has given me some miraculous moments. I have learned that this path is not for everyone, that it takes a warrior's mind and extreme devotion to find true love for yourself. And I know if you are ready to have an extraordinary life filled with love, happiness and success, that it is possible.

—AUDREE

Leadership And High Performance

THE CRITICAL NEED for *Emotional Science* became clear to us when we began working with corporate executives and company leaders. Although the book is written for the everyday person, it is an essential guide for anyone who wants to operate as an effective leader. When unhelpful emotions are showing up at work, you simply cannot operate at your best. Even "minor" emotions such as irritation, annoyance, or feeling unsettled can have a major impact on performance.

High-performance organizations develop leaders at all levels of the organization. A key way of growing the capability of leaders is to increase their ability to work with emotions. We include this work in our leadership training programs.

Leadership goes beyond the corporate world. We all take on the role of a leader at some time in our lives. When we are on a team working with others—whether it is at work, at home with our kids, in our communities, or with our friends—a leader is one who helps the team achieve its purpose. It could be organizing a family vacation, a party, or a community event.

Few are born into 100% supportive conditions since childhood. Almost every one of us needs to learn these essential life skills. *Emotional Science* reveals a practical approach to get to the heart of what is happening with our emotions. From there we can unlock profound success and growth.

Who We Are

Michael

Michael has been on a path of self-discovery and healing for decades to find his own inner peace. By profession he is a leadership coach and trainer. He works with leaders all over the world to develop high-performance organizations through his own integrated system of knowledge, tools, and behavior shifts. He developed this system while helping companies move to an Agile way of working in the software industry.

Michael's graduate work in computer science trained him in sense-making to understand models and theories in a profound way. As an engineer by training, he likes practical structures and tools that can make this world a better place. This way of understanding the world helped him come to terms with himself and his emotions. His outlook brought him to approach emotional growth and healing with the mind of an experimental scientist: "Show me the data to prove that!"

Audree

Audree's quest to liberate herself from pain and suffering led her to study the psychology of disease. With over 10 years of formal training as an energetic healer, including meditation and yoga, she became an expert in personal growth and transformation.

Audree's natural abilities to sense energy and read people has been effective in her career as an energetic healer. As a member of a medical team for 5 years, she had high levels of success with "untreatable" diseases, such as Stage IV cancers (brain, breast, and ovarian), addiction, depression, anxiety, chronic pain, life transition, and cases of identifying hard to diagnose illnesses. Her work has been scientifically validated and recorded.

Audree's career in medical healing shifted as she began to have awareness of the correlation between disease, lifestyle, and consciousness. She studied as a professional coach and developed techniques to quickly remove blocks and obstacles that keep one from living to their fullest potential. Today she guides executives and entrepreneurs to clear personal blocks in performance, conducts leadership training, and coaches executives worldwide.

Audree has been a radio host with her acclaimed *Grounding Meditations For The Shift In Consciousness* and is co-author of *The Authorities*. She has been initiated by beings in very high states of consciousness to guide her clients through deep processes that create lasting shifts in consciousness.

The Sahotas train and coach worldwide on conscious leadership, organizational culture, and the behavior changes leaders need to deliver high performance.

Michael and Audree have a passion to change how we live in the world. It is ambitious, yet simple. When there is a shift in consciousness of the leader, this shifts the entire organization. Imagine an organization filled with engaged, motivated, and productive people. This positively impacts not only the workers and the quality of the products they deliver, but also the families and communities the people live in. The ripple effect continues to the partners the company works with and the customers that use their products. So organization by organization, the world will shift to a better place. It starts with leadership.

Although they come from radically different backgrounds, their common vision for shifting the consciousness of the planet is the goal that unites them. Together their tools empower others to facilitate their own healing process. They have both studied extensively at O&O Academy in India, where they met, fell in love, and were later married.

CHAPTER 1.

Get Ready To Experiment

THE HUMAN CAPACITY for emotions is vast. Emotions can be both positive and negative. Some positive emotions are happiness, excitement, and love, to name a few. The positive emotions create sensations in our being that feel good and allow us to have connection with the world around us. Negative emotions such as anger, fear, jealousy, and hatred keep us separated or disconnected. Emotions are a pervasive part of life experience and they are an aspect of our humanity. They are also responsible for how we relate to the world and how we are interconnected with it. They have a great impact on how we create our reality and how we respond to experiences. Our negative emotions have a destructive impact on our experience of life. We will explore the negative consequences of emotions in this book.

As human beings our reality is shaped by our emotions. Emotions impact the way we live our lives. Negative emotions prevent us from living life to the fullest. They stop us from living our highest and greatest potential and restrain us from taking risks and living our purpose. Negative emotions keep us in separation and disconnection to life and the relationships that make up our experiences. They keep us trapped and imprisoned in rules and past conditioning.

When you are free and clear from carrying negative emotional burdens, you are more resourceful on every level. With emotional awareness comes the truthful examination of what is there. Working through your emotions will increase your ability to respond as opposed to spending time in an emotionally triggered state.

With your negative emotions engaged, you are not your authentic self. When in an emotional charge you can be loud, judgmental, or unrelenting with your opinions. Or you can remain quiet and reserved when it is in your best interest to speak up. You may show up in a certain way that does not reflect what you actually believe. This creates damage within ourselves, destroys our teams, and toxifies our relationships.

Are you ready to achieve the success you desire? A life where you have healthy relationships and extraordinary results? Being at peace with your emotions is the first step toward acceptance and freedom. Instead of being stuck in the life you *don't* want—a life filled with stress, worry, arguments, negativity, tension, and fear—you can live in peace, happiness, and fulfillment. By relaxing into your emotions you can learn to embody a joyous and successful life.

Becoming aware of your emotions can help you operate in a highly energized way. You can show up resourcefully. You will start to feel relaxed with yourself. You will be able to respond more positively. People will be able to connect with you, because you can better understand yourself. You can speak your truth. You will be able to communicate with others, including those who hurt you, such as your loved ones. Collaboration increases. Inspiration accelerates. Productivity goes up.

Instead of letting the outside world control how you feel, grab the opportunity to increase ownership of your life. Through this work you can create awareness about your emotions and enable clarity. You can learn to accept your emotions instead of fighting and resisting them.

By operating like a scientist for your inner world, these learning materials can help you become conscious of the emotions that are blocking your success. Your ability to regulate your emotions is *critical* for high performance. When we are emotionally clear, we can function more competently and create the change we want to see in life. Stop letting your emotions run your world and start growing so you can get the results you want.

A Note From Audree:

I developed the Get Clear Technique at a time when I was experiencing a lot of unusual emotions. I began waking up in the middle of the night with heart palpitations and experiencing extreme anxiety during the day. There wasn't any obvious reason for this; my life was not in danger, and I really had no reason for any fear or anxiety. I remembered an offhand remark by a teacher in India during a meditation practice to sit still for 49 minutes: "Notice the sensations in your body." I took this conscious awareness of physical sensations and I began a personal practice that lasted over a year. Every morning, for 10 minutes, I sat with the very uncomfortable bodily sensations that came with the anxiety. At first, I thought I was going to die with tight chest pains and a rapid heartbeat. Although I had been hospitalized for these symptoms 8 years prior, I allowed my body to have the sensations and told my mind to let go. I started to notice that as I practiced this "technique" my symptoms began to subside before the 10 minutes were up. It became easy to sit and breathe into the uncomfortable bodily sensations and they dissolved rather quickly. I soon noticed that if I had anxiety during the day, I would stop what I was doing and begin to breathe into the bodily sensations. The symptoms would soon dissolve within a few minutes.

I began to use this technique with my clients. They would have a thought or feeling, I connected it with a bodily sensation they were having and I would guide them into this breathing technique. My clients would experience a relief or cessation of the symptomatic response to their emotions.

When I met Michael, he had already been working with his emotions and this practice was of great interest to him. We began working together with this technique, bringing him into a deeper awareness of his emotions and a quick release using the Get Clear Technique.

We both use the technique on a regular basis and have guided our clients with this work. Our wish is to find fast and easy techniques that provide successful, healthy outcomes.

How To Get The Most Out Of *Emotional Science*

Quite simply, you can connect with your own experience of how your emotions work and then begin to understand them and shift them. You can become in tune with your current belief system so you can see how it is impacting you and your current view of the world. Whether it is at work, at home, or in any relationship, implementing the tools in *Emotional Science* can help you create the shifts you need to show up more effectively.

The information offered is not a theoretical approach. It is a direct, applicable practice grounded in everyday reality that anyone can do.

We offer easy to use models to help you connect with your own inner experience. This includes step-by-step exercises in dealing with negative emotions as they arise. It also incorporates tools for shifting emotions that are causing difficulty. These exercises, infographics, and illustrated diagrams will help you develop emotional awareness.

The practices will help you notice the difference between the emotions you experience in the moment and the negative charges that get stored in your body. You will start to be able to recognize past conditioning and unhelpful behavioral patterns that keep you locked in a current state of suffering and the low performance that comes with this.

The learning traditions for this work are quite diverse: neuroscience, modern psychology, Eastern spiritual traditions, and Neuro-Linguistic Programming (NLP). We, Michael and Audree, continue to be the primary test subjects; all of the material used is developed and continually experimented on us first. Many experience profound healing with this information and by applying these practices; including friends, family, and clients who welcomed the help and proven methodologies. The results have been tremendous.

How To Achieve The Best Results

The exercises presented are comprehensive and can be used for ongoing emotional health and wellness.

For the first time through, follow the chapters in chronological order. This is important in order to achieve maximum benefit. Return to the material as frequently as possible. For example, many people use some part of the material for a daily, weekly, or monthly practice.

IMPORTANT: Exercise Booklet—Free Download

This book has many written exercises that are critical for understanding and integrating the concepts. If you want to get the full benefits, we encourage you to pause and complete the written exercises.

You can either write in your book or download a free Exercise Booklet PDF from our website.

Go to **www.emotionalscience.com/download**
and enter the code: **freedom**.
We will email you the information.

Play Full Out

For best results we highly encourage you to play full out. You will get out what you put in. Go as far and as deep as you possibly can. Do this not just the first time you read it, but each and every time you pick up the book.

All of these practical structures are available instantly and can be used any time, anywhere you are. However, we recommend that you perform the activities in a space where you feel most safe. This can be in a private room or a secluded area. Have no outside distractions. Allow no one around that can divert you. Turn off your cell phone. Do not drive or operate heavy machinery while performing the exercises.

Most of our emotions are developed when we are young, often before we have language. Therefore it is extremely effective to draw what you are going through as there will often be no words to sufficiently or adequately explain your feelings. For the exercises, have blank paper beside you to draw whatever pops into your mind. And, for maximal efficacy, we highly encourage you to use color markers.

Write anywhere within the pages. Using color markers, pens, sticky notes, permanent markers—mark up the whole book. Fold the edges, rip out the pages or stick them on your wall or fridge. You have complete, 100% permission to use this book in any safe manner possible in order to acquire optimum results.

As you read through you are encouraged to keep a journal. Take notes about your insights and feelings and record any other observations. Date your notes so you can always come back to them and see how much you have grown. Many of the exercises are designed to help you realize your current belief system so you can see for yourself if your ideas are clear. Document your thoughts as they arise since most of what you are sensing is keeping you at your current level of performance.

One trap that some people fall into is the practice of "spiritual bypassing." Spiritual bypassing is when people go from emotional pain to joy and bliss without exploring their emotions or deeper sensations of suffering. Although it allows one to escape the pain, it also prevents growth. *Emotional Science* is your ultimate companion and friend. Go deep and use it fully.

Exercise Set-Up

Below are instructions for how to get ready for the exercises in this book. Please follow these instructions for each exercise. The following instructions are in detail to give you an understanding of the importance of each step.

Step 1. Find a quiet place.

This is to bring you into an environment where there are no distractions or disruptions. Cell phones are off or on silent with a "Do Not Disturb" sign on your door. Inform people around you who might require your attention that you will be having a few minutes offline or that you are meditating.

Step 2. Read through the exercise.

At this step it is important to read through the exercise *before* you actually do the exercise. Most of the exercises are best experienced with your eyes closed. Reading through the exercise first will give you a better understanding of what to do. For ease of practice we have free of charge audio recordings for each exercise found on the *Emotional Science* website at www.emotionalscience.com.

Step 3. Have your back straight and your feet flat on the floor.

This is the optimal position for the exercises. Laying down during the exercises will increase the likelihood that you will fall asleep. It is also recommended that you do your best not to move your body during the exercises, as movement creates distractions. If you do move, such as with an itch or a cough, just become aware of the timing; the mind and body will create distractions to keep you from processing memories or bringing up emotions. For example, an itch or body movement will pull you out of a meditative state or come at a time when you are experiencing an uncomfortable memory to prevent you from growing.

Step 4. Close your eyes and breathe deeply.

There is no right or wrong in having your eyes open or closed. We recommend that your eyes are closed to have a deeper experience. If you feel more comfortable with your eyes open, find a spot to focus on, about 3 feet in front of you. Rest your gaze on that spot and continue with the instructions.

Breathing deeply is a simple way to quiet the mind and relax the body. Take a deep breath to inhale and then exhale as slowly as you can. Keep all your awareness focused on the breath. You can bring your awareness on the rise and fall of your chest or the rise and fall of your abdomen (belly). Repeat this 3 times at the beginning of each exercise to relax and center yourself.

You may want to bookmark this page for further reference. We will have reminder "set-ups" before each exercise.

Self-Care

Here are some practical guidelines for self-care while exploring your emotional landscape.

- Hydrate; drink lots of water.
- Get lots of rest.
- Do not operate vehicles or heavy machinery for at least 1 hour after each exercise.
- Be gentle with yourself.
- Do not watch scary or violent movies after performing any of the exercises (you will be open and vulnerable).
- If you experience strong emotions:
    - Lie down flat on your back for 10 minutes on a yoga mat, on a bed, or just on the floor. Keep your arms at the sides

of your body, palms facing upward. Close your eyes. Breathe. Relax. Allow yourself to become aware of your abdomen rising slowly and falling with each breath.
    - Cover yourself with a blanket.
- Avoid conflict.
    - If you are having difficulties with someone, it is best not to interact with them for at least 24 hours after any practice.
- Do not make any life-determining decisions.
    - After emotional clearing, you may receive insights and clarity that could cause a sudden urge to make drastic changes in your life. Wait at least 1 week before embarking on any life-altering decisions.

Who Should *Not* Read This?

Emotional Science is *not* intended for those who are interested in an academic read of how emotions work.

This is not an instructional guide about how to change the states or behaviors of others. What you will receive is the secret of great influence — by changing how you show up.

Does This Stuff Really Work?

If only by desiring, thinking, and wishing the problems and challenges in our life to go away were really that easy, all of our problems and challenges would disappear overnight. The reality is that we can't wish them away.

Although application of this book is intended to help you develop your consciousness and grow, we acknowledge this is only one avenue for arriving at your own truth. This instrument of personal growth has helped us on our path, and today we share it with you.

This work is about understanding yourself. It is for becoming aware of your own internal workings. It is for anyone who wants to show up more resourcefully, wherever they may be. It may be used to develop your capacity as a parent, leader, or as a partner and friend.

> *May you benefit from this body of work so that you live through the fullness of your being. May you learn to express your truth and break away from suffering and live an extraordinary life.*

CHAPTER 2

Your Emotional Truth

MOST OF US are not completely aware of our emotions. It turns out the typical societal beliefs we have about emotions keep us locked in a state of unhappiness. But through the process of becoming aware of our own beliefs, we can become unstuck. This is why it is imperative to have a clear understanding of our beliefs. This chapter will assist you in clarifying those beliefs.

Our societal beliefs about how emotions work is incomplete and even misleading. This will only present itself once you invest the time to see how you currently experience reality.

We will take you on a journey to discover how you experience emotions and what you believe about how they work. Understanding your current beliefs is critical for preparing your mind so you can truly contemplate changes.

Let's Clarify Your Understanding Of Emotions

At this moment you are here with your thoughts and beliefs about how the world operates. That is natural. We all have views about how that happens. Within our current understanding of reality, we have a set of beliefs around emotions and how they work.

When a new piece of potentially relevant data emerges, we are designed to first evaluate whether or not it is of value to us. Something is said, and immediately we decide if we want to believe it. The idea is either rejected or accepted. Our mind is continually picking and choosing what it thinks it should believe. This is done in order to survive.

When it comes to a new idea — especially one that is intended to help you grow — it is much easier to say, "No, I don't agree with that." The mind will reject an idea when it is different from existing beliefs. This is so because the brain is designed to stop thinking as soon as possible when a new idea tries to come in. In order to understand your emotions you will have to put in extra effort to learn and grow the new neural pathways required to see things in a different light.

Your openness to learn and listen to new ideas will determine how quickly you will grow.

It's time to investigate your current set of beliefs about emotions.

Exercise:
Your Emotional Understanding

Exercise Set-Up
1. Find a quiet place.
- No distractions or disruptions.
- Cell phones are off or on silent.
- Make sure you are undisturbed. For example, inform people around you or that require your attention that you will be having a few minutes offline or that you are meditating.

2. Read through the whole exercise.
- It is important to familiarize yourself with the exercise so that you know what to do when your eyes are closed.

3. Have your back straight and your feet flat on the floor.
- Use a chair.

4. Close your eyes and take 3 slow breaths.
- The best way to take a slow breath is to inhale and exhale slowly and equally.
- Do this with all your awareness focused on the breath.
- Notice the rise and fall of your chest.
- Do this slowly and fully 3 times.

Exercise Steps: Your Emotional Understanding

1. Contemplate how your emotions work.
- Eyes closed.
- Take a few minutes to reflect on your emotions as per the questions below.

2. Write down answers to the following questions.
- Open your eyes and write down answers to the following questions.

Where do emotions come from?
Answer: _____

What are emotions?
Answer: _____

How do emotions block you in your current life?
Answer: _____

How do people or situations cause you to have emotions?
Answer: _____

How effectively can you control your emotions?
Answer: _____

Identify your current beliefs by reviewing what you have written above.

What do I believe about emotions? _____

_____

_____

Now take a moment to check in with your comprehensive set of beliefs you have around how emotions work. Circle your answers to the questions below—no answer is right or wrong. Your job is to answer truthfully. When you can answer honestly, you will get better results. You will see where you are.

My emotions never get the better of me

Strongly Disagree   Disagree   Neutral   Agree   Strongly Agree

Other people can make me angry

Strongly Disagree   Disagree   Neutral   Agree   Strongly Agree

I need to control my emotions to live a happy life

Strongly Disagree   Disagree   Neutral   Agree   Strongly Agree

There are things I can do to shift my emotions

Strongly Disagree   Disagree   Neutral   Agree   Strongly Agree

My thoughts influence my emotions

Strongly Disagree   Disagree   Neutral   Agree   Strongly Agree

I can feel emotions in my body

Strongly Disagree   Disagree   Neutral   Agree   Strongly Agree

Exercise:
Your Emotional Belief System

Notice your answers to the questions in the previous exercise.
Review what you have written. Look at your answers.

The answers to your questions in the Your Emotional Understanding exercise define your emotional belief system. You have a set of beliefs about how emotions work.

The question is: where did you get this belief system? And…is it truthful?

Is it possible that your belief system is not actually based on the truth of how your emotions work?

How do you know if your belief system is right? Let's find out.

Exercise:
How Well Do You Understand How Your Emotions Work?

1   2   3   4   5   6   7   8   9   10

(Circle your best answer as quickly as possible. Your first instinct is the most accurate.)

10: You are 100% clear about how emotions work. You understand exactly where they come from. You know how they relate to your thoughts. You are absolutely certain about how they work. You have nothing new left to learn.

1: You don't understand. It could be that examining your belief system seems quite confusing. Or you may understand how you think about emotions, but have no idea if you are right.

Diagram 1: Do You Understand Emotions?

If you have a low score: you are all set to learn from this book. It means you are ready to let go of your existing beliefs to find something that serves you better in your life.

If you have a high score: you have a great start to unraveling the truth and are ready to jump right in.

Where are you truthfully? How well do you understand where your emotions come from? How well do you understand how they work and how they shift? The key is in being honest with yourself. Being dishonest with your real score will only get in your way. To create the change you want in your life it is important to start with the truth of where you are, not where you want to be.

What Do We Normally Experience?

We are often disconnected about where we are emotionally. Most of us were never educated about our feelings. We learn to function as though there is an external world *without* emotions, and believe *that* is reality. At a basic level, social norms dictate what is considered acceptable. We adopt socially acceptable ways of operating. We live in a society of emotional denial and disconnection. Our misunderstanding of our own emotions keeps us locked in perpetual misery and dissatisfaction.

Most of us have also been taught to *manage our emotions*. *Controlling* or *managing* our emotions is actually a severe form of disconnection, or a way of avoiding what is really going on. You may fear that if you reveal your hurt, anger, or sadness that there will be no end to it. You may have been taught that crying is a sign of weakness. You may think that arguing is better than no interaction at all. If your family is used to being silent and inexpressive or avoidant in front of other people, then you may have learned to do the same.

Or you may have experienced your emotions taking over when relating to others. Possibly you grew up in an overly emotional environment where negative or violent emotions were the norm. You may now frequently experience negative emotions. Perhaps they are unavoidable and uncontrollable. You seem to react emotionally and create disconnection to situations and others.

Experiencing emotional discomfort is a normal part of being human. Our nervous system is very flexible and adaptable, and shapes the way we respond to reduce suffering. It adapts itself to all situations. Our emotional system is constantly adjusting itself to allow us to adapt to whatever conditions we are in. For example, if there is a lot of love then we will be very wired for connection; and if there is an absence of love, then we will be more wired for protecting ourselves. It is very brilliant, the way our nervous system is designed. What it really comes down to is your individual level of sensitivity and what happened during a situation. This is an entirely normal and natural process that impacts all of us.

If you have completed the exercises so far, your own ideas about emotions are becoming self-evident. Everybody has a different emotional truth based around their own beliefs.

We will now introduce an experientially proven model to help you understand the structure of your emotional system. Please check it out. Understanding how emotions work can allow you to become disentangled from your current cycle of pain and suffering. When we live in a place of truth, we can stop letting our emotions run our lives.

CHAPTER 3

Emotions: It's Not What You Think

IN CHAPTER 2 we helped you unpack your ideas about your understanding of emotions. To receive the full benefits of this material you have to complete the previous chapter, including the exercises.

We are bringing you into a very different way of understanding your emotions. It is so different that it requires firsthand experience. The following exercises lay the groundwork for exercises in later chapters when you learn to shift your emotions. There may be times you will want to walk away from this book, or you may be telling yourself the ideas here are not true. At these times be open and aware that you may be at a point of breakthrough. During these moments the mind will want to stop to avoid change. Just notice when this happens and then decide whether to take a break or keep going.

Now that you understand your existing beliefs about emotions, it is time to increase your awareness of how your emotional system actually works.

In this chapter you will be guided through your own discovery of how emotions work. You will act like a scientist or explorer on the inner workings of yourself. This way you will know for sure it is true and not just a theory.

How Does Your Emotional System Work?

Most scientific and progressive psychological theories tell us that our emotions are neurological responses. They are generated in the body, giving us information about the world we live in. This information is then available for further processing, which we can then use to determine our next action. Our emotional system helps us to survive so we can react to events around us that are perceived as threatening to our survival.

Although this way of seeing the world might be true, it is important to have an experiential understanding of how our system works. It is less helpful to have labels or a logical understanding. The reality is that language does not truthfully and accurately convey what we are feeling. There are common experiences that are useful to describe, and language is one way to point us in the right direction. But when it comes to the human experience, there is really an unlimited list of what could be going on and many things happening in complex combination.

Describing and categorizing our emotions is like trying to describe all the colors that exist. How many colors are there? Well, if you look at the color palette, there are infinite colors. Similarly, the human experience is limitless. To discover this deeper part of ourselves does not come from the use of logic or language. It must come through our inner experience.

We will now take you through a series of exercises so you can have an experiential understanding with your emotions. Each exercise will guide you through your own emotional system. Remember to be honest with yourself. Go as deep as you can.

We are going to start with the basics to make sure we are on the same page about how we experience reality.

Exercise:
Emotions Happen

Let's start by checking to see how you experience emotions and explore how they appear in your life.

Think of 3 situations where you noticed your emotions.

Situation	Thoughts	Emotion/Feeling In Body
1.		
2.		
3.		

Table 1: Emotions Happen

Situation: What was happening. The context of the incident.
Thoughts: What were your thoughts about the situation?
Emotion/Feeling In Body: What was the feeling inside of your body while this was happening? For example, tightness in your jaw, clenched stomach.

What we invite you to notice is:

When something happens we have
THOUGHTS + FEELINGS.

Diagram 2: Something Happens, We Have Thoughts And Feelings

Sometimes we get curious and wonder: which comes first? The thoughts or the feelings?

Our advice is not to worry about this. It turns out that we can get emotional clarity and a better life without answering this. So, let's leave it for Eastern mystics. All you need to notice from the results of the exercise is that something happens and then we have thoughts and emotions about it.

When you are ready, we now invite you to experience a happy memory.

Exercise:
Happy Memory

Exercise Set-Up
1. Find a quiet place.
- No distractions or disruptions.
- Cell phones are off or on silent.
- Make sure you are undisturbed. For example, inform people around you or that require your attention that you will be having a few minutes offline or that you are meditating.

2. Read through the whole exercise.
- It is important to familiarize yourself with the exercise so that you know what to do when your eyes are closed.

3. Have your back straight and your feet flat on the floor.
- Use a chair.

4. Close your eyes and take 3 slow breaths.
- The best way to take a slow breath is to inhale and exhale slowly and equally.
- Do this with all your awareness focused on the breath.
- Notice the rise and fall of your chest.
- Do this slowly and fully 3 times.

Exercise Steps: Happy Memory
1. Think of a happy memory.
- Eyes closed.
- Take 1–2 minutes to experience the memory fully.
- Pause and take note of the sensations. Relax into the memory. Let go of any impulse to change anything.
- Notice the physical sensation in your body right now. Put your hand on that part of your body where you feel something and breathe deeply into that area.

2. Write down answers to the following questions.
- Open your eyes and write down answers to the following questions.
- Stay connected with the feeling.
- As you answer the questions, you may need to close your eyes to connect with your inner experience.

How do you feel right now? Record your observations.

Observations:

Hint: There are infinite ways to describe your experience. For example:
- I am feeling warm and happy.
- I laugh when I think about this.
- I can see it like it was yesterday.
- I can remember exactly what they said.

Notice the* physical sensations *in your body.

Where are you feeling it? _____

What is the texture? _____

What is the color? _____

What is the temperature? _____

What does it feel like in your body? _____

*Does it feel like this experience is
happening RIGHT NOW?*

↓

Yes / No

> **We now unlock a key secret about emotions.**
>
> ***You are recalling the past.
> And it feels like it is happening right now.***

You know the feeling is coming from the memory. Not the book. Not the place you are in this present time.

**Even though it feels like it is happening right NOW,
it is actually a feeling from the past!**

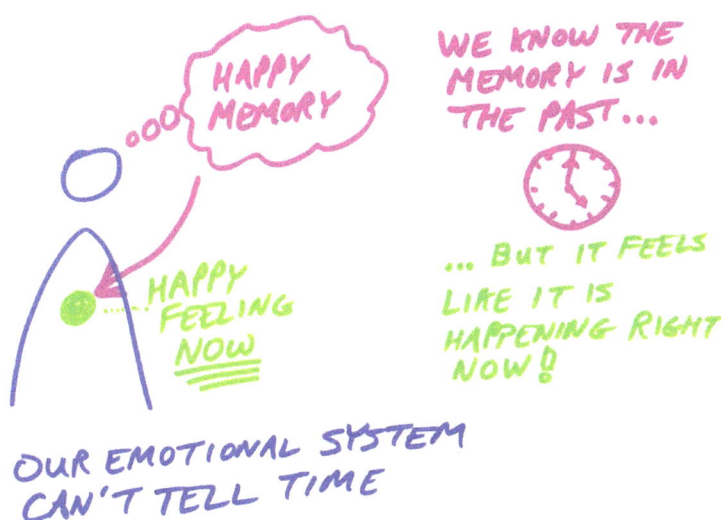

Diagram 3: Our Emotional System Cannot Tell Time

Our emotional system *cannot* tell time.

Our emotional system cannot differentiate between the past, present, and future. It cannot tell if what you are experiencing is happening right now or if it is something that has *already* happened. So when we bring in a happy memory from the past, it actually feels like it is happening to you right now.

Our memory recall system *can* tell time.

Our memory recall system encodes time. When we recall a memory we can tell that it is from the past—not right now. We never get confused that a memory is happening right now; we always know it is from the past.

While going through the Happy Memory Exercise you may have experienced feelings of warmness and tingling, happiness, laughing, an uplifting sensation of openness, calmness, or warmth expanding throughout your chest area. Your senses were activated and you might have sat up straighter. You may have "seen" visual images in your mind's eye as if they were happening right there and then. You may have started to even "hear" people and noises and remember exact dialogue and conversations. **You would have also felt physical bodily sensations.**

Generally, your senses were activated. **Although your experience is caused by something that happened in the past, it felt like you were reliving the same thing all over again in the present moment.** There was nothing you were doing that was causing those physical sensations. This is all normal and happens when your emotional and recall system are functioning properly.

If you are wondering to yourself, "Is this really true? Can it be that my emotional system really cannot tell time?" If so, we have a bonus exercise just for you.

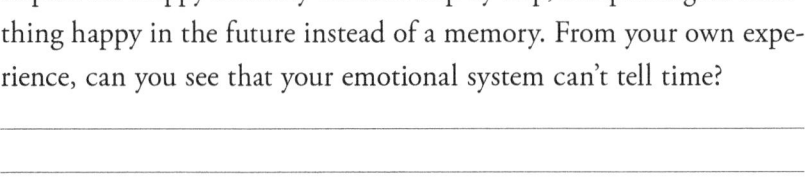

Repeat the Happy Memory Exercise step by step, except imagine something happy in the future instead of a memory. From your own experience, can you see that your emotional system can't tell time?

___

___

___

Now Let's Explore Challenging Emotions

Now that you understand the basics about emotions, you are ready for the next series of exercises.

If we only remember happy memories all the time, then the world would be wonderful. We would be happy. All the time. Can you imagine what it would be like to be happy all the time, no matter what is happening around us?

That is not our reality. Our reality is that challenging emotions come up: fear, anger, frustration, jealousy, worry, and anxiety, to name a few. They feel unpleasant. We do not like the sensation of these emotions in our bodies. In order to master them, we first need to learn about them and understand them. So let's dive in.

Where Emotions Hijack Us

Have you ever noticed someone with a strong emotional reaction to a situation?

For example, your spouse might come home after a long day at work and starts getting angry and frustrated, and there's nothing that is outright happening that can explain this behavior. Or someone at work gets really mad for what appears to be "no reason."

Let's start by looking at how challenging emotions show up all around us.

Exercise:
Other People's Reactions

From an observer standpoint, someone else's reaction might seem completely absurd and irrational. A situation happens and for that person it feels as though it is the end of the world (and for them, it actually is). A situation might put a damper on their whole day or preoccupy their whole week. Sometimes they might even bring something up from the past, from months or even years before. When people have strong emotional reactions, it might appear as if they are in their own world or "crazy"—or at least over-emotional about a situation, or unreasonable and you cannot relate or speak with them. Have you ever experienced a person who has an incredible amount of drama in their life?

We often try to connect with people who are in an emotionally charged state to help them calm down. We might say any of the following, but they will have little effect:

- "I can't understand why you get so upset by something that's no big deal."
- "Why can't you just chill out?"
- "Relax."
- "Take it easy."
- "Whoa. Calm down."
- "There's no need to overreact."
- "You're overreacting!"
- "Can't we just talk about this?"
- "I don't understand why you're so upset."

People who are in an emotionally charged state don't seem to listen to logical reasoning or understand something when you try to explain to them what is going on.

Think of 3 situations where someone you know had a strong emotional reaction that didn't make sense.

Situation	Action	Emotional State	Calm Action
1.			
2.			
3.			

Table 2: Other People's Reactions

Situation: What was happening. The context of the incident.
Action: What did the person do? How did they act?
Emotional State: What emotion(s) was this person experiencing? How intense were the emotions?
Calm Action: What might someone who was calm have done in that situation? How would that have helped?

Hint: Here are some situations that might trigger a strong emotional response:
- Traffic.
- Politics.
- Arguing about who is right.
- An unjust situation.
- Partner not responding.

Choose 1 of the 3 situations in Table 2 and circle it.

A. How intense was the person's emotional response?

1   2   3   4   5   6   7   8   9   10

A score of 10 is VERY INTENSE.

B. Did the situation threaten their survival?
Was their life in danger?
Was their existence on this planet threatened?

1   2   3   4   5   6   7   8   9   10

(10) being 100% YES: meaning someone is just about to take their life and their existence is about to end. They are going to die.

(1) means that they are actually okay. They are alive, uninjured, and they are in no immediate danger. They are going to survive.

Compare A and B.

Chances are, your answer to A was much different than B. It's very easy to see that people's reactions can be way out of proportion to what is happening around them. People react as if it is life or death about situations or events that are really not that significant in the grand scheme of things.

There is very little that we actually experience that is a true threat to our first-world experience—that is all future stress that we are creating for ourselves, which is actually created from the past.

*Some emotional responses are completely
out of proportion and out of relationship
with the events that are actually happening.*

All we are doing here is noticing a discrepancy between how we feel and what is really happening around us.

Now examine the remaining 2 situations you described in the previous exercise. Do you see how other people's emotional responses had a high level of intensity compared to the logical significance of the event?

Let's Examine Our Own Behavior

It is easy to notice another's reaction, but harder to tell when it is happening to you. So how do you know if *your* reactions are proportionate to the circumstances? Let's do another exercise to find out.

The only way to understand how your emotions work is to look into your own experience. We are asking you to look at challenges because there is no other way to get into the learning.

This brings us to the next exercise:

Exercise:
When Life Hits Us

Exercise Set-Up
1. Find a quiet place.
- No distractions or disruptions.
- Cell phones are off or on silent.

- Make sure you are undisturbed. For example, inform people around you or that require your attention that you will be having a few minutes offline or that you are meditating.

2. Read through the whole exercise.
- It is important to familiarize yourself with the exercise so that you know what to do when your eyes are closed.

3. Have your back straight and your feet flat on the floor.
- Use a chair.

4. Close your eyes and take 3 slow breaths.
- The best way to take a slow breath is to inhale and exhale slowly and equally.
- Do this with all your awareness focused on the breath.
- Notice the rise and fall of your chest.
- Do this slowly and fully 3 times.

Exercise Steps: When Life Hits Us

1. Think of a situation where you had a strong emotional reaction.
- For this exercise please use a situation with **moderate intensity**.
- Eyes closed.
- Take 1–2 minutes to experience the situation fully.
- Pause and take note of the sensations. Relax into the memory. Let go of any impulse to change anything.

2. Write down answers to the following questions.
- Open your eyes and fill in Table 3: When Life Hits Us.
- As you answer the questions, you may need to close your eyes to connect with your inner experience.

3. Repeat for the other 2 situations.
- Repeat Exercise Steps 1–2 for 2 other situations.

Emotions: It's Not What You Think   33

	Situation	Action/Behavior	Thoughts	Emotion/Feeling In Body
1.				
2.				
3.				

Table 3: When Life Hits Us

Situation: What was happening. The context of the incident.
Action/Behavior: What did you do? How did you act?
Thoughts: What were your thoughts about the situation?
Emotion/Feeling In Body: What was the feeling inside of your body while this was happening? For example, tight jaw, clenched stomach.

Now Let's Do An Emotional Reality Check

Diagram 4: Emotional Reality Check

When something happens, there are thoughts and feelings. You learned this earlier. Now we invite you to ask yourself the same questions we asked you when looking at other people's behavior. Let's go!

Choose 1 of the 3 situations in Table 3 where you had a strong emotional reaction and circle it.

Remember the situation fully. Close your eyes. Allow yourself to fully experience it.

A. How intense is this feeling right now?

1   2   3   4   5   6   7   8   9   10

A score of 10 is VERY INTENSE.

B. Does this threaten your survival?
Is your life in immediate danger?
Is your existence on this planet threatened in this very moment?

1   2   3   4   5   6   7   8   9   10

(Circle what best describes the feeling.)

(10) being 100% YES: meaning someone is just about to take your life and your existence is about to end. You are going to die.

(1) means that you are actually okay. You are alive. You are uninjured. You are in no immediate danger. You are going to survive.

Compare A and B.

Chances are, your answer to A was much different than B. Just like with other people. Some of our emotional responses are completely out of proportion with the severity of the events that are happening.

Asking yourself these questions provides a powerful way to identify the level of disconnect between what you are feeling vs. how threatening something actually is.

Now examine the remaining 2 situations you described in Table 3: When Life Hits Us. Do you see how your emotional response had a high level of intensity compared to the logical significance of the event? Now examine your life. By this reflection, can you see how this pattern has been running in your life? Can you see how you have experienced strong emotional reactions that didn't really fit the situation you were in?

Relax. It's normal. That's how we are wired as human beings.

Our emotions are running our lives!

It is easy to see when other people behave or react in a way that is out of context, but it is not always clear to see when it is happening for us. The path of growing is to **Stand in the Truth** of where we are and recognize our behavior. It is not about changing what is happening, but noticing what is really going on. The moment we become aware of what is happening within ourselves we will be able to move forward.

Imagine how your life would be like if you were able to deal with life events *without* a strong emotional reaction. This is what we will be learning in the next few chapters.

Notes: What If I Can't Access My Emotions?

1. What if there is no memory?
You may or may not have full or complete memory of a particular situation. As a defense mechanism our nervous system closes off access to many of our painful memories to avoid re-experiencing the intense pain over and over again.

If you do not have a memory recall, it is okay. The feeling will show up somewhere in your body as a bodily sensation (for example, a tight feeling in the stomach, clenched jaw, or a rapid heartbeat).

Please note: If you are experiencing very extreme physical sensations for more then 20 minutes, please contact your physician or medical facility.

2. What if I can't get a feeling in my body?
Sometimes intense situations can cause the inability to access physical feelings in the body. Although we do recommend you continue with the exercises to the best of your ability, you may need more support than what is offered in this book.

3. What if I have used an experience of abuse? How does this help?
There are times or periods of abuse in many people's lives. This book is not therapy, nor can it or will it tackle any questions of how to deal with these traumatic experiences. From exploring *Emotional Science* you should be able to identify a pattern of abuse, yet will that be sufficient for you to stop it? If you see these patterns, please step out of the role as victim by seeking professional help. We say this with utmost compassion, and implore you to personally take this most responsible action of self-care.

CHAPTER 4

Emotions 101: How Emotions Work

IF YOU HAVE completed the exercises in the previous chapters, you have done the work to your fullest ability and you have made it here, you are over halfway there. Now we're going to help you understand how emotions block you.

In Chapter 3 you explored how you experience emotions through a series of exercises. Let's unpack them.

Unpacking The Experiments With Emotions

First, you noticed that when things happen in the world around you, you have thoughts and feelings. Then you discovered through the Happy Memory Exercise that your emotional system cannot tell time. And sometimes there are strong emotional reactions that don't make sense. Let's tie these together.

> **Things happen, and then there are thoughts and feelings.**
> **Our emotional system cannot tell time.**
> **We have strong emotional feelings that do not make sense.**

Something happens in the world around us. We have thoughts about it. We notice a feeling inside our body. For example, someone cuts you off while driving. You start thinking about the situation: "What a jerk! That guy thinks he owns the road!" You may notice a feeling in your body — a clenching in your abdomen, perhaps; and you also notice that you're really angry. You became aware of your symptoms in the last chapter.

What's going on here? You are experiencing an emotional response that is completely out of proportion with the events that are actually happening. It doesn't make sense that you would have such an intense reaction to a normal, everyday event such as experiencing someone's poor driving. The current situation does not warrant such a strong reaction.

Now let's pull together what you learned about your emotional system not being able to tell time. So where does this strong emotional reaction come from?

There is only one place they can come from — *the past!* Yes, it turns out that your emotional system works just the same way for positive emotions as it does for challenging ones.

Strong emotional reactions in the present are caused by emotions from the past.

We tend to believe that it is the current situation causing the emotion. This is where our irrational behavior comes from.

Our brains are pattern-matching machines that sort information very quickly. In order to process information to keep us safe from what it perceives as danger, the brain functions at its highest level of efficiency by finding already established neural connections. There are many theories and evidence that proves this. What matters in your growth and learning is that you discover for yourself if it is true.

The brain assesses incoming information and finds a pre-existing neural pathway that is similar to a previous situation. Therefore it saves time by utilizing an already established pathway. The brain will then define and detect what it perceives as danger much faster. What the brain does not do is recognize that the situation or event is new and different. It will compare the current situation with one from the past —one that matches—as guidance on what to do.

What happens when a situation matches a repressed memory—a memory that is blocked from conscious awareness? It can still exist in our emotional system, yet we will have very little, if any conscious awareness of it. We tend to believe that it is the current situation causing the emotion. This is where our irrational behavior comes from.

Executive Coaching Example

Michael and I were coaching an executive on a day he was going to have an important meeting with his team. The exec was sharing how frustrated the last few years had been; that the same conversations were repeated over and over, with no decisions being made. As the exec was speaking, he was getting angrier. We both could see very clearly that the reaction of anger had nothing to do with the leadership team and the issues the exec was sharing with us. However, to this exec it was very clear that the frustration and anger was about the current situation and that his leadership team had stagnation and indecision. We also knew this exec could never have clear communication and productivity with the leadership team while holding a reaction of anger and frustration.

In the next 5 minutes we worked with this client to identify and express the anger and frustration. Next I asked, "Who does this remind you of?" The light bulb went off and he responded, "My father."

It was in that moment that this executive knew deeply that the behavior of the leadership team triggered his anger about his father's behavior. This awareness allowed the exec to take a step back from the situation and see what was going on. Later that day we received a text: the meeting went well even though the same behaviors of the leadership team were present. Our client had a completely different reaction—no anger. This created an opportunity for a more productive meeting with less stress and turbulence for our client.

So here is how your emotions work: when a challenging situation comes up, so does an unconscious memory of a similar situation and the emotions that were stored with that event. You feel like those emotions are happening right now. Just like with a happy memory.

But since you don't recall it in the moment, your brain thinks the challenging emotion has to do with the current situation and makes you act as if there was a strong, challenging event happening to you in the present.

Of course, it is also possible that you can sink into the feeling and re-experience the actual memory of when that emotion was caused. **Whether you can remember the exact experience is not relevant for healing and growth.** If you do remember the event, then you already have your own proof that you are acting out of the past—just like the Happy Memory Exercise and our example with the executive.

Not every memory is positive. Memories that are from unpleasant, negative experiences are more likely to be buried and forgotten by our consciousness. They are buried deep in the subconscious. For the purpose of this book we will address these subconscious and stored negative memories.

The diagram below ties this all together.

Diagram 5: How Emotions Work

Let's recap what usually happens to us:
1. **Something happens in the present.**
2. **We notice we have thoughts and feelings.**
3. **We mistakenly think that the feelings are based on the current situation.**
4. **We assume that the current situation is causing the feelings.**
5. **We act in the present based on our past emotions and struggle with life.**

To get what we want in our lives we need to respond to what is happening from a resourced place; **a place of calm where you have access to intelligent actions.** When there is an emotional reaction, we are not resourced. We are not intelligent. In fact, the opposite happens: we are at our worst. In this way our emotional reactions are preventing us from living the lives we want to lead.

Before we talk about how to use this understanding for creating a new way of life for yourself, let's look into what exactly are these negative emotions from the past.

What Did I Just Experience?

We already identified earlier that our emotional system cannot tell time, yet our recall (memory) system can. As you learned in Chapter 3, positive emotions can be re-experienced and enjoyed as they float through us. We can bring in a happy memory and it is as though we are living through it all over again.

But what happens with emotions that we struggle with?

Sometimes we may be in situations when the emotions *can't* flow through us. Unlike a positive emotion that you identified with the Happy Memory Exercise, an emotion we struggle with may not fully go through our system. "Stop crying!" someone might shout at us when we are young, and whatever we were feeling gets *stuck*. **When there is no space to fully experience the emotion it becomes repressed or lodged within the body.** We call these trapped or locked emotions *emotional wounds*.

You identified strong emotional reactions already from the experiments in Chapter 3. These reactions are from *emotional wounds* **and are unrelated to the present situation.**

Emotional wounds are critical to become aware of. When an emotional wound is activated, you become unresourceful. You react in a way that does not necessarily reflect what you believe. You act in an unintelligent or overly-emotional way.

Emotional wounds are what cause setbacks, blockages, obstacles, or roadblocks and spontaneous emotional reactions. Being able to understand what they are and how to recognize them when they show up is key to unlocking the results you want.

What Is An Emotional Wound?

An explanation can help us orient and calm down the mind a bit. But in reality, **an *emotional wound* is something we can only experience in our bodies.** We can only experience emotional wounds through our beings and in our bodies. The mind can only do the thinking, and the wholeness of our being is not a thinking thing.

So to calm the mind down we can describe **an emotional wound** as *an unprocessed emotion that lives within the body.* We can also use similar words to direct ourselves toward the same experience:

Unprocessed emotion.
Trauma.
Repressed feeling.
Subconscious.

All these descriptions point toward the same thing. It is not about whether one term is right or more correct than the other. Using language to describe your experience only serves as a signpost to point you in a certain direction. What is really happening is a **felt body-sense; a real-time feeling in your body** even though it is something you experienced in the past.

We prefer to use the term "emotional wound" because words like "trauma" tend to trigger people right away. Other words seem to cause analysis-paralysis or overthinking, generally resulting in internal mind chatter and unnecessary self-debate. **An emotional wound is simply something in our being—a hurt that is there.** When we experience situations that we can't handle, the emotions get stuck and stored in our bodies and nervous system. It is a blockage that just sits there.

An **emotional wound** *is an unprocessed emotion from the past that lives within the body.*

How Do Emotional Wounds Get Created?

Let's take some time to understand how emotional wounds are created. For the purpose of healing and growth, it doesn't really matter how they originated. But it does help to explain them in order to orient our conscious minds.

For example: imagine you are a little kid, playing or minding your own business and then something happens that shocks your system.

We have an experience that we can't handle and our system arranges itself in a way to reduce our pain and suffering. We are complex and adaptable systems, created for efficiency and survival.

For example, when the physical body gets injured, the muscle tissue quickly begins to form temporary criss-cross patterned tissue around the area to protect it. This tissue forms a "knot" and it affects the functioning of the muscle. The muscles around the injury also tighten up to protect the wound so no other damage occurs. Although the body is creating these patterns for strength and support, the injured body part functions in a degraded way. Our nervous system does the same thing with our emotions. Defenses form around emotions and they are tucked away and hidden until they reveal or express themselves. And we operate in a degraded way.

Our nervous system is built to seek pleasure and help us avoid pain.

Because an emotional wound elicits a *negative* emotion, when it is being activated we are experiencing pain—psychological pain. Just like a physical injury, if we are experiencing pain then there is an immediate desire and aspiration to have that pain leave us.

> *We do whatever it takes to cut off the pain*
> *so the source of suffering stops.*

Under average circumstances we do not recognize we are experiencing an emotional wound of the past so we try to change the world outside of ourselves. We blame situations, people, things, or take part in some sort of self-destructive behavior—all to stop the pain. Disconnection is also a really good move to avoid what is really going on.

> *Simply put: emotions are experienced in the moment.*
> *The wounds get stored.*

Traditional Chinese Medicine (TCM) understands this and expresses it very clearly:
> *Emotional activity is seen as a normal, internal, a physiological response to stimuli from the external environment. Within normal limits, emotions cause no disease or weakness in the body. However, when emotions become so powerful that they become uncontrollable and overwhelm or possess a person, then they can cause serious injury to the internal organs and open the door to disease. It is not the intensity as much as the prolonged duration or an extreme emotion, which causes damage.*

Once physical damage has begun, it is insufficient to eliminate the offending emotion to affect a cure; the prolonged emotional stress will require physical action as well. ...[Emotions] represent different human reactions to certain stimuli and do not cause disease under normal conditions.[1]

How Does An Emotional Wound From The Past Show Up In Your Present Reality?

We do not feel okay when we are re-experiencing our wound.

So how can we recognize when an emotional wound is being expressed or re-experienced? Here are some words that can help direct you:

Charge.
Emotional hurt.
Trigger.
Internal struggle or conflict.

Again, these are just words to help point you to an **internal body experience.**

A common example of an activated emotional wound is when someone changes a plan, or changes the timing for a meeting—especially

---

1. "What Are The Seven Emotions?" Shen-Nong Ltd., 2006, www.shen-nong.com/eng/principles/sevenemotions.html.

at the last minute—and your immediate response is to get frustrated or annoyed. During this type of situation any painful (lodged) memories and unfulfilled emotional needs and desires will start to surface as a strong emotional response. You might feel angry and resentful. Then you start putting destructive energy into the situation and cause emotional damage for yourself and your relationships.

Once we notice we are in an emotional wound, we can realize, "**Oh, right! I understand what is happening. I am reacting this way to a situation because something here is activating an emotional wound within me.**" Then you can start to shift your attention inward rather than going outside of yourself to "fix" the world outside and resolve things.

An emotional charge is a strong emotional response.

When an emotional wound activates, we experience an emotional charge.

Common Coping Mechanisms
- Pretending everything is always okay (operating from denial, looking the other way or turning the other cheek, general avoidance behavior).
- Taking recreational drugs or alcohol (covering up or numbing the pain).
- Overeating or undereating.
- Setting up distractions or diversions; being constantly busy.
- Becoming a workaholic.

Emotional Wound = Limiting Belief

Usually an emotional wound comes with a limiting belief. In addition to a feeling in our body, there is a belief that we have about the world that limits how we can perceive and interact with it.

Here are a few examples:
- "The people I experience closeness with always end up leaving."
- "The people who love me will always betray me."
- "When people ignore me, I am not worthwhile as a human being."
- "When people interrupt me, that makes me feel that what I have to share is of no value."

We will explore how these show up inside of ourselves in the next chapter. For now, let's look into how they operate in our lives.

Dr. Gabor Maté, a physician specializing in neurology, psychiatry, and psychology, explains what happens with emotions by pointing out what occurs if you call someone a **"green bush."**[2] That is exactly as it sounds. This means that we are a shrub-like plant that is green. How would you respond if someone called you that? It is generally meaningless. It makes zero sense and would probably only bring up a few mental images. We certainly will not get angry. Why? We know we are not a green bush. We are so sure that we are not, we would decide the other person was mistaken or confused.

However, if something is said that we think may be true, there can be emotional wounds and beliefs around these statements. For example, if we call someone "thoughtless" or "lazy," we will typically

---

2. Gabor Maté, "Compassionate Inquiry" (seminar, Toronto, ON, Canada, November 3-4, 2016).

get a strong reaction vs. calling them a "green bush." The reason we have this reaction is that somewhere inside we actually have the belief that we are "thoughtless" or "lazy." If we did not have this belief about ourselves—if we truly believed that the opposite was true, then other people's words would have no effect on us. We would just think the person is mistaken or confused. Just as if they called us a "green bush."

Imagine we have an emotional shock to our system when we are very young. We make up a belief to encode information on why this is happening so we can prevent it from occurring in the future. Makes sense in theory, but in practice what happens is **we end up with a lot of beliefs that are not true.** How does this happen?

For example, you are an infant crying in the crib and no one comes. At that moment, you might make up the belief, "There is no one who really cares about me," to explain what is happening and to ease the psychological suffering. Our minds are very young and make up a story (or belief) on the spot to explain what is happening around us. It doesn't need to be true or even make sense as an adult. It just needs to make sense to the mind of a child.

How We Create Our Own Reality

How do we create reality? **We see reality through the lens of our beliefs.** For example, if I believe, "There is no one who really cares about me," then I will look to prove this in all my relationships. Rather than seeing how people actually care about me and love me, I will look for things to show that they don't. I will be unable to see the larger picture because it does not fit within my worldview.

Stop Acting Like A Child

Imagine you are acting from an emotional wound; the wound that was created when you were a child, and now active in the present. As a result you will be acting from the age that the wound was created. 2 years old, 3 years old. How effective do you think you will be? That's right. You will be as effective as a 2 or 3 year old. This is why we create damage to our lives and to our relationships when we act out of an emotional wound. Literally all the intelligence and learning of our lives is thrown away in favor of a temper tantrum. This is the plain truth of what is happening. So there is only one thing to do: "Stop it!" It may seem a little harsh, yet truly effective. We'll talk more about how exactly to do this in Chapter 5.

Re-Experiencing Emotional Wounds

Think of a particular challenge that seems to happen in your life over and over again. It may show up as a problem you can't seem to solve. It may be a similar type of situation that's happening repetitively. Perhaps there is a lesson you thought you already learned, but the same type of circumstance is still showing up. You may ask yourself, "Why am I in this situation again?"

For example, you keep having the same conversations over and over, and some things keep eliciting a strong emotional charge. Or similar situations keep happening—sometimes with the same person, sometimes with different people. For some reason it does not seem to matter which direction you go, because you run into the same type of problem eventually.

When an emotional wound is activated, you experience a strong emotional response or charge. Just like a physical injury, an emotional charge is like scar tissue that has formed around the wound but the injury itself hasn't completely healed yet. When life hits us, the unhealed wound gets irritated and the wound becomes activated again and again.

Let's look at Table 4 to see how an emotional wound activates an emotional charge.

TIME 0 →	TIME 1 →	TIME 2 →	TIME 3 →	TIME 4 → ... etc.
ORIGINAL EMOTIONAL WOUND CREATION	Re-experiencing Emotional Wound	Re-experiencing Emotional Wound	Re-experiencing Emotional Wound	Re-experiencing Emotional Wound

Table 4: Emotional Wound Time-Lapse

Let's unpack the same table in further detail to tie everything together.

TIME 0 →	TIME 1 →	TIME 2 →	TIME 3 →	TIME 4 → ... etc.
ORIGINAL EMOTIONAL WOUND CREATION	Emotional Charge	Emotional Charge	Emotional Charge	Emotional Charge
SITUATION: My father yelled at me. 5 years old.	Incident: My baseball coach (male) scolded me.	Incident: My uncle shouted at my aunt at the dinner table.	Incident: My boss (male) forcefully demanded something of me.	Incident: An older man yelled at someone across the street from me.
THOUGHTS: "I must be a really bad person. I did something wrong."	Thoughts: "I must have been doing something wrong."	Thoughts: "I hate him. He is a really bad person. I must stop this. I don't know what to do to make things right."	Thoughts: "What a jerk. I can't believe this guy. I can never do anything right. This is the kind of stuff I have to deal with at work every day."	Thoughts: "This person is so loud. He must be a really bad person. Why does he have to shout like this? I wish he would just shut up."

Table 5: The Effects of Emotional Wounds Over Time

(Continued) Table 5: The Effects of Emotional Wounds Over Time

TIME 0 →	TIME 1 →	TIME 2 →	TIME 3 →	TIME 4 → … etc.
BODILY SENSATION: An empty hole in my stomach.	Bodily Sensation: My stomach felt like it was punched.	Bodily Sensation: A tight ball squeezing in my stomach.	Bodily Sensation: Like there is a clenched knot in my stomach.	Bodily Sensation: As though someone is jabbing my stomach.
IMMEDIATE REACTION: I pulled away, agreed, obeyed, stayed quiet and didn't say anything.	Strong Emotional Reaction: I pulled back and obeyed him, even though it felt wrong and I didn't agree.	Strong Emotional Reaction: Staying quiet, remaining at a distance, avoiding family dinners and extended family functions.	Strong Emotional Reaction: Slamming items around, complaining about him to other people. I do not put much effort into my work.	Strong Emotional Reaction: Walking away even though I wanted to say something. I later criticized his behavior to my friends.

Where do emotional wounds get stored?
Answer: in the body.

If the emotional wound becomes experienced again and again, after enough times **some sort of belief starts to form around it.** "**When people do x, then it means y.**"

Let's look at some other examples.

Example 1: Julie

Julie grows up without knowing her father. The emotional wound (TIME 0) gets created in response to her father leaving. Julie starts feeling a sense of "abandonment."

When Julie turns 13 she falls in love with a boy. He rejects her (Time 1). Since that feeling-sense of abandonment lives within her, whether she is fully aware of it or not, the original emotional abandonment wound is re-activated. Understandably, Julie has a strong emotional response to the incident, which causes her continued suffering. After a few days, this all dissipates. She continues on with life, a little more cautious than before.

Time goes on. Julie gets married after experiencing multiple break-ups (Time 2). At 45 she divorces (Time 3). During the divorce deep feelings of abandonment begin to resurface again, this time more severely. She begins to seriously question whether or not she can ever "keep" a man and wonders "if all men are the same."

Over time she starts acquiring multiple beliefs about herself and how the world works based on that original experience. She starts to believe her thoughts that she is "not good enough" or that "nobody loves her." She goes so far as to believe no man can ever be trusted and as a result becomes single for the rest of her life.

Julie starts to believe she can never have another relationship. Her beliefs around that feeling-sense of abandonment are lodged so deep that it is infused with her personality.

Julie's reality is shaped to avoid the painful experience of being "abandoned."

In this way, by living her life to avoid that feeling-sense of abandonment, Julie's emotional system is protecting her from experiencing pain and suffering.

Example 2: Rob

As an adult Rob notices that he doesn't really feel like he can rely on anyone. It becomes a real problem for him since he experiences difficulty working on a team with others and feels it is almost impossible to work with contractors or staff who report to him. He runs into challenge after challenge trying to get projects done since things keep going wrong: delays, poor quality work, and being unable to depend upon a project's completion.

When he was young, his father said, "99% of humanity is stupid," and, "if you want something done properly, you have to do it yourself."

Imagine for a moment how it must feel for Rob when his father made those judgments. As a child, Rob started to believe that he was the person that his father was speaking about. As a result he repeatedly experiences his father's judgment and internalizes this as an emotional wound with the belief, *"I am not good enough."*

In Rob's life, he constantly tries to prove he is good enough. To get recognition, he works hard to be better than others. But no amount of success or recognition can fill this emotional wound.

His almost desperate desire to succeed leads him to take on the same judgments about others—that they are "not smart enough" and "can't do a good job." And then this becomes true—since his unconscious mind continues to search for ways to prove its authenticity. Instead of looking for people around him succeeding, he looks for all the ways they are wrong and making mistakes. Everyone can pick up on this and does not really want to work with him, so they don't put the effort and care in. In this way, we can see how Rob creates his own reality.

How does Rob break out of this cycle? He simply starts to notice when he has judgments about others. He stops to notice the discomfort—the emotional wound—which he experiences as a tight pressure across his chest and a tight, sick feeling in his abdomen. This happens every time he works with someone else.

This is why emotional wounds can actually prevent us from living the life we want to live. In the examples above, Julie may never be able to experience the fullness of love from a man because of the pain associated with the beliefs around the experience of her father leaving and the need to avoid that feeling of abandonment. We can go even deeper to say that this emotional wound may also cause issues with any man seen as an authority figure or in a role as a mentor or leader. Similarly, Rob will likely never be able to build successful teams and relationships if he fails to notice the ongoing negative cycles he is in.

*You **become** the wound; you act out of the emotional wound. It is a part of your beliefs and controls the way you live and respond to life.*

What If There Was No Emotional Wound?

Imagine something happens but there are no emotional wounds around it. How will you react? The answer is: you will just respond to what is happening—there will be no emotional charge around it.

When there is no emotional attachment, all is clear. When there is no emotional wound there is no charge around a situation. For example, you can be at a place where someone is late or changes plans and there will be no strong emotional reaction; no emotional damage. There is no hurt. You can use your full intelligence. There is only a rational response focused on living a happy, productive life: *What shall I do while I am waiting? Hmmm...this person may not make it to our meeting...what do I want to do with this bonus time that I now have?*

What Do You Believe?

At this point we will pause and ask you to reflect on your beliefs around emotions. If you do not believe the model shared here, ask yourself: what is the other credible model that explains your emotional reactions? If you do not believe this is actually happening, then what other methods are you using and what are you actually believing? And how else do you explain reality? What is your current understanding? Test it out with your own experience and see what happens.

We are constantly experiencing emotional wounds from the past. Having awareness of this creates so much more space where we can respond more positively. The importance of moving through difficult emotions is to help us come to the reality of what is happening and be able to live from a place of acceptance and truth. The alternative is that we are acting out of emotional wounds and making unintelligent choices that are not in alignment with the way we want to live our lives.

So if we did not *create* a situation that caused an emotional wound within us, and we cannot just change our negative emotions through our own willpower—what steps can we take to move through this, not with our minds, but with our beings?

The next chapter will guide you through your negative emotions so that they can become released. Only then can you start to live from your highest potential.

CHAPTER 5

Working With Emotions

In this chapter, we introduce the Emotional Freedom System and how you can use it to become more intelligent when faced with an emotional challenge. Through repeated application, you will be able live more of the life that you want.

How We React To Life

Let's start with a review of how we react to emotional charges.

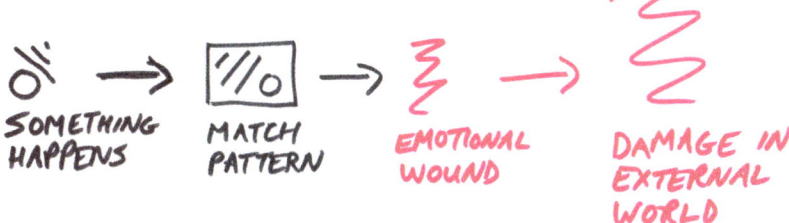

Diagram 6: Life As Usual

Diagram 6 is a recap of how emotions run our lives. Let's walk through this:

1. **Something happens in the external world.**
2. **Our nervous system matches the pattern as best as it can to decide what to do. In the drawing, you will notice the pattern is not exactly the same as the external event. The brain finds a close pattern match. This is how we start distorting reality and losing our connection to what is really happening.**
3. **A memory is activated that triggers an emotional wound.**
4. **We act from the emotional wound and create damage in our external world.**

This is usually how we live our lives—reacting automatically to the emotional wounds that come up in daily life. **It is not the emotional wounds themselves that cause damage, it is our reaction to them.** Let's look at how we can react more intelligently in the face of negative emotions.

Introducing: The Emotional Freedom System

The Emotional Freedom System is a set of interconnected practices that are used to break out of reactive emotional patterns. There are 3 key components to this system. We will explain each of them in the following chapters.

Diagram 7: Emotional Freedom System Summary

There are 3 distinct parts to the Emotional Freedom System to support your success:
1. **Emotional Freedom Checklist:** Use the checklist to understand your emotional reactions and to stop causing damage.
2. **Get Clear Technique:** Use this to clear a negative emotion that is blocking you from responding in an intelligent, resourceful way.
3. **Enhanced Emotional Awareness:** Use the 4 Traps Of The Mind to increase your ability to escape from destructive behaviors.

When used together on a daily basis, they will support tremendous personal growth and a healthy, productive life. Increased self-awareness and acceptance are the keys to mastering your emotional landscape.

A Deeper Truth

Viktor Frankl discovered a deep truth while he was in a World War II concentration camp. In his book, *Man's Search for Meaning* he observes:

"Between stimulus and response there is a space. In that space is our power to choose our response. In our response lies our growth and our freedom."[3]

Here is how we can apply the Emotional Freedom System to live the life we want.

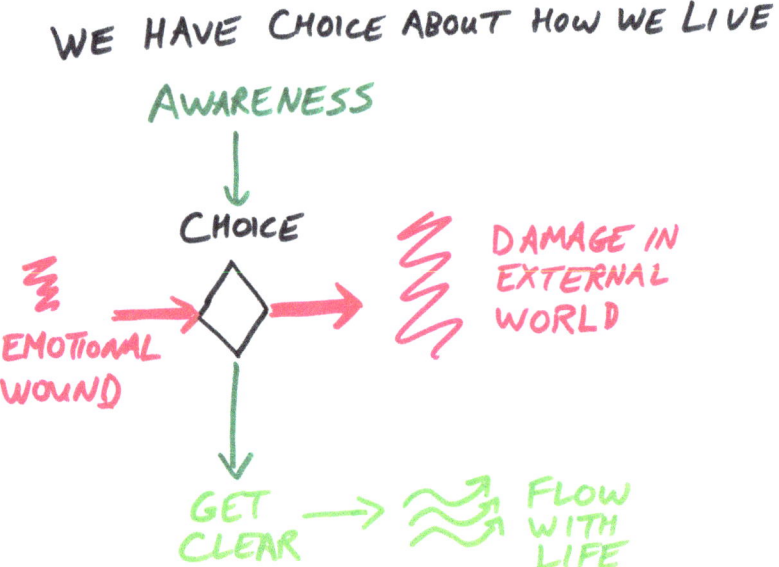

Diagram 8: Awareness And Choice

When you are experiencing a charge from an emotional wound, your default behavior is to react and cause damage in the external world. You are conditioned to respond this way. The thick red arrows in

---

3. Frankl, Viktor E., *Man's Search for Meaning* (Boston: Beacon Press, 2006; first published in German under the title *Ein Psycholog erlebt das Konzentrationslager*. Original English title was *From Death-Camp to Existentialism*, 1946).

Diagram 10 denote that you have strong neural networks in place to make this happen. In many situations, you are stuck in a rut or in a groove like on a record.

With the Emotional Freedom Checklist and the Enhanced Emotional Awareness tools, you can bring yourself to a place of choice. In that choice lies your freedom. You can apply the Get Clear Technique to get into a more resourceful state so you will be able to flow with life to create positive outcomes, achieving high performance in all areas of your life.

Now that you have an understanding of the overall approach, let's dive into each one of the elements of the Emotional Freedom System.

CHAPTER 6

Emotional Freedom Checklist

IN THIS CHAPTER, we introduce the Emotional Freedom Checklist to limit the damaging effects of your negative emotions. We will introduce you to 7 steps that you can use to orient yourself so that you stop causing damage when you are in an emotional charge. Going through the following 7 steps will help shift your perceptions of reality. You will become more resourced and function at a higher level to create greater levels of success.

To learn how to use the checklist, you will go through this chapter TWICE. The first time, read through the checklist so that you have an understanding of each step. The second time, you will apply the checklist to work through an emotional charge you are actually experiencing.

As you practice this and learn how to work these steps, you will be able to quickly reference them every time you want to get freedom from an emotional response that is blocking you. As you gain mastery and while you are in a presenting situation that is emotionally charged, you will go through the checklist internally and quickly.

Here is what you need to do NOW:
- Read through the entire chapter to get an intellectual understanding of this material.

- Go through the chapter in an experiential way where you connect with an emotional wound and practice the checklist step by step.

Exercise Set-Up
1. Find a quiet place.
- No distractions or disruptions.
- Cell phones are off or on silent.

2. Have your back straight and your feet flat on the floor.
- Use a chair.

3. Close your eyes and take 3 slow breaths.
- Inhale and exhale slowly and equally.
- All your awareness is focused on the breath.
- Notice the rise and fall of your chest.
- Do this slowly and fully 3 times.

4. Alternate between reading and feeling.
- Open your eyes to read the instructions and steps below.
- Close your eyes to connect with your inner feelings and sensations.

Instructions: Connect With An Emotional Charge
- **Connect to a *negative emotion* right now by examining an area of conflict or lack in your life. When we say *"right now"* we mean that you can feel it in your body.** If you are unsure what will trigger you, take a refresher look at the Chapter 3 Exercise: When Life Hits Us.
- *The only way to learn is by doing. You must work through an emotion as you read this to learn the practice.* **Go through each step slowly and completely.**
- Write the emotional charge down in your notebook or draw it right now.

Checklist:
Emotional Freedom

Step 1:
Stop And Notice The Negative Emotion

The first step is very simple: **just stop what you are doing and *notice* that you are experiencing a negative emotion.** You might say to yourself: "Wow. I am experiencing a lot of anger right now." **Just** *acknowledge* **it.** No need to change it. Just observe it.

Step 2:
Observe The Physical Sensation

Now observe exactly what is going on in your body: what physical sensations are you actually experiencing?

What does it feel like in your body?

Location: _____
Temperature: _____
Texture: _____
Color: _____
Other: _____

A. How intense is this feeling right now?

1   2   3   4   5   6   7   8   9   10

(Circle what best describes the feeling.)

A score of 10 is VERY INTENSE.

Step 3:
Check To See If The Emotional Response Makes Sense
Let's check in with the level of danger that you are feeling.

B. Does this threaten your survival?
Is your life in immediate danger?
Is your existence on this planet threatened in this very moment?

1   2   3   4   5   6   7   8   9   10

(10) being 100% YES: meaning someone is just about to take your life and your existence is about to end. You are going to die.

(1) means that you are actually okay. You are alive. You are uninjured. You are in no immediate danger. You are going to survive.

Compare A and B.

Notice if your emotional response is out of line with what is actually happening around you.

Ask yourself: "Does the intensity of the emotion make sense with the level of danger I am in?" At this moment you can acknowledge to yourself that **you are in an emotional overreaction that has nothing to do with the present moment.**

When you can notice a strong emotional response, this same awareness will begin to dissolve the reaction. The observation of a behavioral pattern causes a disruption in the pattern.

Step 4:
Accept That It Is An Emotion From The Past

Look at what is happening and say out loud to yourself the following statements:
- What I am experiencing right now, in my body, has nothing to do with what is happening now.
- I am experiencing an emotional wound from the past.
- All I can do is **accept** that the wound is here right now.
- Changing what is happening around me will not fix my emotional wound.

A critical step to understanding your emotions is accepting them. There is nothing to change. The first step is to accept that there is an emotional charge that is connected to an emotional wound.

*It is when you are in resistance to what is happening that causes struggle
and difficulties in your life.*

"Awareness is 67.8% of healing."
— Audree Sahota

Once you are looking at the truth of how you are, the growth process begins. When you have no awareness of what is happening or you are in self-deception, there is no hope for growth.

Step 5:
Stop Trying To Change The Present

Now that we have been looking at our inner world and accepting the emotional wound, we can stop trying to change the world around us to make the problem go away. We know it won't work. We know the emotional pain we are experiencing is a result of the past. The present is only triggering a memory, not actually causing the suffering.

*"My suffering has nothing to do with
the present moment."*

*It is a deep acknowledgement that there is no
situation or person causing my suffering.
It is mine alone based on my past.*

With this deep realization, we can stop blaming others for our suffering and stop causing damage in our relationships.

For example, when someone says something that hurts, we can fully realize that the feeling of hurt comes from the past. Instead of focusing on them, or demanding they say sorry or telling them they are wrong, we recognize that they are just a trigger for a past hurt. And blaming them will not fix the hurt. Remember the "green bush" insult?

Step 6:
Stop Reacting From The Emotional Wound

We act at the maturity level of growth we were when the wound was created. So when we are in a wound that happened at age 3, we act like a 3 year old. **How effective is relating to another from an emotional wound?** How much damage and harm will we cause when we are reacting from this place?

Our recommendation around responding while re-experiencing an emotional wound is very simple:

Don't respond while you are in an emotional charge.

It will only cause harm to you in your life when you react from a place with low ability to respond.

You are far more likely to get to positive outcomes when you have all your intellectual resources available to you.

Emotional Responsibility is…
Choosing to act only from an emotionally clear space
Or not to act when in an emotional charge

Decide How You Want To Show Up To Your Life (Relationships, Work, Etc.)

1. Respond while this emotional wound is actively charged
2. (and likely cause damage to both yourself and the other people involved).
3. Wait until it subsides and respond with full awareness and intelligence.

The choice is yours. The success you want to create for yourself rests in each time you make this decision. You determine how you show up in all areas of your life. The way you "show up"—your behavior and responses to situations and people around you—becomes the makeup of who you are. It determines the quality of your personality and in turn, determines the quality of how you lead your life.

A common anger management technique is to:

Take a timeout.

This applies to any emotional charge, as well. If you are in the middle of a meeting or conversation, you can simply let people know that you want to continue, yet you are feeling a strong emotion and need to take a break for a little while. If it is not possible to take a break, notice your reactions, pause, and breathe. You can process the situation at a later time. The pause will allow you to stop reacting in the moment, regroup, or stop any damage.

What if you can't take a timeout?

Here are some simple tactics to help:
- Take more time before responding.
- Breathe into the feeling while the meeting is proceeding (more on this in the Get Clear Technique).
- Master these techniques so that you can quickly use them in any presenting situation.

Step 7:
Let Go Of Identification
Now that you have taken the decision to look inward at your emotions, **the next step is to notice how the mind creates identification with the feelings that you experience in your body.**

The only real truth is that you are experiencing physical sensations in your body. Anything beyond that is a fiction created by your mind.

Let's take a look:

**Just observe the difference between your
thoughts vs. the actual emotion
and the physical sensations that accompany the emotion.**

"I am sad."
"I am frustrated."
"I am afraid."
"I am feeling upset."
"I am angry."
"I am jealous."

**Anything with "I AM" is not an actual emotion.
It is a thought.**

Our thoughts create reality. When you think, "*I am sad*," you reinforce the feeling of "sad." The alternative is to examine the feeling and explore what is actually there.

Your emotion is not actually *you*. It is just a physical sensation in your body. This is important to internalize.

Emotions are not you!

Emotions are physical sensations in your body. Your emotion is not actually *you*. The emotion is a reaction based on past experiences.

And there is something even more astonishing here: **emotions are labels we create to describe physical sensations in our bodies.** You have already experimentally verified that you have physical sensations. What you are calling your emotions are just labels. So whose labels are they? Emotions are thought of as collective, shared labels.

> *"Your emotions are not your emotions."*
> —Michael K Sahota

It is through our identification that we are claiming the emotions. When you let go of the identification and labeling of the emotion, you are free to focus on the physical sensations.

Working With An Emotional Charge

We recommend that you follow all of the 7 steps of the checklist before you can start to release the emotion through the Get Clear Technique. The most important on the list is Step 7: Let Go Of Identification to the charge and the wounding itself. This is the *"choice"*—where you choose to show up in a different way.

Summary:
The Emotional Freedom Checklist

This is a checklist to fast-track the work. Use the Emotional Freedom Checklist below to notice when you are in an emotional charge and recover from it.

1. Stop And Notice The Negative Emotion
2. Observe The Physical Sensation
3. Check To See If The Emotional Response Makes Sense
4. Accept That It Is An Emotion From The Past
5. Stop Trying To Change The Present
6. Stop Reacting From The Emotional Wound
7. Let Go Of Identification

CHAPTER 7

Get Clear Technique

IN THIS CHAPTER, you will learn the Emotional Freedom System's Get Clear Technique to clear an emotional charge so that you can flow with life. Once you have gone through the Emotional Freedom Checklist, you will have disidentified with your emotional charge and you are ready to let go. Now is the time to release the charge very quickly.

The technique below will take you through your emotional charges, clearing them quickly without going back into the "*story*" of "why" they are there. This clearing exercise is for you when you are ready to let go. You have chosen to release what no longer serves you and you have decided that you are ready to get the success you want in life. You want to access your full intelligence to perform at your best.

Warning: The practice you are about to experience will feel uncomfortable. As you practice this technique, you will become accustomed to the experience and it will become more familiar and agreeable.

It is helpful at times like this to remember the spiritual teaching:
"No pain, no gain."

Get Clear Technique:
Get Ready

Read through the following instructions to familiarize yourself with the steps before undertaking this practice.

Warning: A reminder that the work in this book is not medical advice. If you are experiencing abnormal physical symptoms that are more than just emotional, please seek medical attention. You should not experience intense physical sensations for more than 15 or 20 minutes. If you have any heart or psychological conditions, you should consult a physician before undertaking this practice.

<u>**Set a timer for 10 minutes**</u>.
<u>**Only do this exercise for 10 minutes**</u>: If the emotional charge does not go away, repeat again the following day.

Find a quiet place to sit with your back straight and your feet flat on the ground. This practice works best if you are sitting in a chair — avoid lying down.

Get Clear Technique:
Steps

1. Take 3 slow breaths.
- Inhale slowly with all your awareness focused on the breath.
- Breathe in and out.
- Bring your awareness to the rise and fall of your chest.
- Do this slowly and fully 3 times. (Take longer if you need to settle in.)

2. Bring awareness to your body.
- Feel your body sitting in the chair.
- Feel your feet flat on the floor.
- Feel your chest rise and fall with your breath.
- Feel into your body.
- Feel for physical sensations in your body…just noticing physical sensations.

3. Feel the emotional charge.
- Bring into your awareness the emotional charge.
- Identify the physical sensation in your body from the charge.
- Bring all of your awareness to the physical sensations in your body.
- It will begin to get uncomfortable.

4. Breathe into the bodily sensation.
- Breathe into the physical sensations…into the discomfort.
- Allow the sensations in your body to intensify.
- Keep breathing into the uncomfortable sensations until the timer goes off.

(10 MINUTES).

What To Expect

As you go through this exercise, the bodily sensations may become extremely uncomfortable…stay with it. **This is the KEY to succeeding.**

Sometimes an emotional charge can clear within 5 minutes. Even if the charge has cleared, continue to breathe for the full 10 minutes. You will know the charge is clearing by the lessening of the physical sensations.

Sometimes charges are very intense and you will feel the intense bodily sensations for the full 10 minutes. In this case you will have to practice multiple Get Clear Techniques to work through this emotional charge. This is normal.

As you go through this exercise, you may notice that your mind will wander or you will be distracted. This is normal. The mind is designed to pull you away from discomfort. As an example, you may experience wanting to move, or you may have an itch. And this is the way we stay stuck. Just notice this is happening and come back to the physical sensation in your body.

Guided Audio

You can follow the instructions above, or you can download the guided Get Clear Technique from the website www.emotionalscience.com/download and enter the code: *freedom*. Note: if downloaded the exercises earlier, you already have access to this.

How Has This Impacted Your Life?

It's for you to have an evidence procedure to prove to yourself that this technique works. Let's check to see how the checklist steps and the Get Clear Technique have changed or shifted the emotional charge.

Now observe again how intense the emotion is:

How intense is this feeling right now?

1   2   3   4   5   6   7   8   9   10

(Circle what best describes the feeling.)

A score of 10 is VERY INTENSE.

Notice if it has changed from earlier. This is your evidence procedure that following these steps is helping you gain freedom from your emotions. Make a mental bookmark that this process helps you feel better. Then the next time an emotional charge comes up, you will have the knowing that this practice will help you get to a happier and more resourceful place.

Daily Practice Of The Get Clear Technique

To gain emotional freedom, it is essential that you practice the Get Clear Technique every day for at least 40 days. This will give you the ability to establish the practice as a habit. As you become an expert at this practice, it will become readily accessible for you to use this exercise, anytime, any place. You will even be able to be in a charge and clear it rapidly while in the middle of a situation.

We practice so that in times of need we have the ability to respond in an effective way. The truth is that mastery requires practice, just like an athlete or a musician.

We know from research that small, easy habits lead to great results.

Here is what we recommend in order to build emotionally healthy habits and practice this skill:
- Pick a regular time of day to practice. Good options are first thing in the morning or at the end of the day.

- Pick and commit to a fixed timebox. We recommend 10 minutes per session. Use a timer.
- **We invite you to create a contract with yourself for a 40 Day Practice.**

40 Day Practice

I _____ (name), hereby commit to myself and to look after myself by creating 10 minutes of daily emotional practice for the next 40 days. In doing so, I will gain mastery of the Get Clear Technique and be able to respond more resourcefully in my life.

How To Get Clear When An Emotional Charge Comes Up

When you have mastered the Get Clear Technique you can use the same steps immediately as charges come up, in the moment. When you become an expert at this, you will be able to very rapidly re-orient your mind through the Emotional Freedom Checklist so that you can go right to the Get Clear Technique. The clearing of your emotional charges will become faster and easier. With this mastery, you will be able to navigate emotional charges and have healthy responses to all situations.

Resistance Causes Suffering

We are all human and with this comes resistance. This often means not wanting to do the work it takes to shift behavior, or not wanting to "see" the emotional charges and emotional wounds.

Situations present themselves for us to *practice* **releasing emotional charges and wounds.** One may even begin to believe that most of our present experiences are only to bring us into an awareness that we have emotional wounds from the past that need to be cleared. After performing the exercises offered here, you may see numerous situations and behaviors that are deeply saturated in reacting from emotional charges and wounds.

It will not always be easy to notice that an emotional wound is activated. The mind will come in and have tall tales to tell of blame and justifications. It is easier to look outside of the self and place blame than it is to look inward and take responsibility for behavior. This is when resistance comes into play. And you will experience this as you deepen your practice. Resistance to having awareness of emotional wounds will happen. This, too, is part of the growth.

Have compassion for yourself. The practice may take time and as you go through these exercises and deepen your understanding, all of this will become easier.

Summary

It is important to understand that everyone goes through times in their life where they have been hurt. Most of these experiences happened to us when we were very young and patterns of belief and behavior were formed. By choosing to become responsive instead of emotionally charged, there is freedom as a result. There comes a time when one can decide to let go of any wounding that has happened to them.

We are not saying that certain experiences are trivial. We also understand that horrible things happen, and we can either become victims of these episodes or we can become perpetrators in turn. We have all been hurt, abused, demoralized, abandoned, etc. It is easier to stay in the pattern of dysfunction caused by the emotional wound than to face it. At some point in time there needs to be a choice to move on; to move through the pain and suffering and let go. This may sound harsh to some, yet standing in truth is critical for growth.

Everyone is searching for a life filled with great health, success, and amazing relationships. There is an opportunity to stand in your power, to be fully present in your life and show up as your incredibly brilliant self, in your fullest potential. Creating extraordinary results starts with looking at the emotional blocks that prevent you from achieving a high performing life.

When one can connect emotional charges and wounds to an inability to function in a healthy way, there is no longer a need to have an attachment to an emotional wound. One can be released from the emotional charge by letting go of the story of how the emotional wound came to be. This is the choice. And the truth is that for some, they would rather stay with the story of being that victim rather than releasing the story and having a life free from suffering. Emotional pain can serve us. Some use it to blame others for not having the career and success they want, or use it to get sympathy from others. Most of us have subtle forms of manipulation to get our way, or try to have the love we want, or excuses for not living an amazing life.

The Get Clear Technique is an easy and practical way to remove the charges that keep you from being resourced. It will help you to function in a healthier way, creating the ability to operate from your fullest potential. We hope that with the exercises given, including the Get Clear Technique, you can make choices that will give you a remarkable and amazing life—one that you deserve, and that is clear from emotional wounds.

CHAPTER 8

Enhanced Emotional Awareness

In Chapters 6 and 7 you learned the first 2 parts of the Emotional Freedom System: the Emotional Freedom Checklist and the Get Clear Technique. These help us when we are aware of an emotional charge. But what if we are not aware?

In this chapter, you will learn the third part of the Emotional Freedom System: Enhanced Emotional Awareness. You will use this to increase your awareness of when emotions are creating challenges in your life so that you can use the Checklist and Get Clear Technique to recover quickly. **This chapter gives practical ways to increase your awareness.**

Increasing Awareness Of Emotional Charges

Earlier we looked at how to respond once there is awareness of an emotional charge. One challenge is that we are often unaware that an emotional charge is happening to us. Our default behavior when a charge comes up is to simply be in the charge and react from that place. In our society, we are not prepared how to notice when we are in an emotional charge. By reading the book so far, you now have a base level understanding of how to notice when you are in a charge.

We are often unaware that an emotional charge is happening to us.

This chapter gives you some easy ways to notice that you may be responding from emotional charges rather than from a clear, resourced, and healthy place.

Take A Breather

You can check if you are in an emotional charge anytime, anywhere. Just close your eyes for 30 seconds, take some deep breaths and notice what it feels like in your body. This is the fastest, easiest way to detect that you are in a charge. This is a very powerful technique to actively check on your inner state. If you want to maintain a high state of effectiveness, we recommend that you actively check in with yourself throughout the day. One client of ours takes 15 minutes before important meetings to check in and clear any charges. This makes him incredibly effective.

Taking a breather is a great way to be proactive about your emotional state, but what else can we do to increase our ongoing awareness?

4 Traps Of The Mind

The 4 Traps Of The Mind are the key ways to detect that an emotional charge is active in the system. We call them "traps of the mind" since this is how we all function. We can't change that. What we *can* change is our awareness so we can take action to restore ourselves to a more functional state.

Here are 4 Traps Of The Mind:
1. **Looping Thoughts**
2. **Caught In A Story**
3. **Arguing**
4. **Complaining And Venting**

Let's explore each trap.

TRAP #1:
Looping Thoughts

Have you ever been in a situation where your mind keeps coming back to the same topic over and over again? Or you keep thinking of solution after solution as you are trying to solve a problem? What about a conversation that you had or are going to have? You repeat the experience over and over again: "Could I have done it differently, or better?" "What if I did this?" "What if I do that?" Your mind doesn't shut off. It keeps you up at night. It keeps repeating the same situation or conversation over and over again.

These are **looping thoughts.** Our thoughts are stuck in a tape loop repeating the same piece of music again and again, or stuck on a repeat button on a song. And we have no control of these thoughts; it's automatic and we believe this is normal. The mind has created its own system to make use of itself. Thoughts, especially looping thoughts, are what the mind uses to justify its own existence.

Looping thoughts are an indication that an emotional wound is active. The mind uses thoughts, such as looping over and over, to distract our awareness from an emotional wound.

These looping thoughts are an indicator that you are in an emotional charge caused by an emotional wound.

There is no way you can resolve your emotional charge by thinking. It won't help. The only thing that will help is looking at the emotional charge feeding the thoughts.

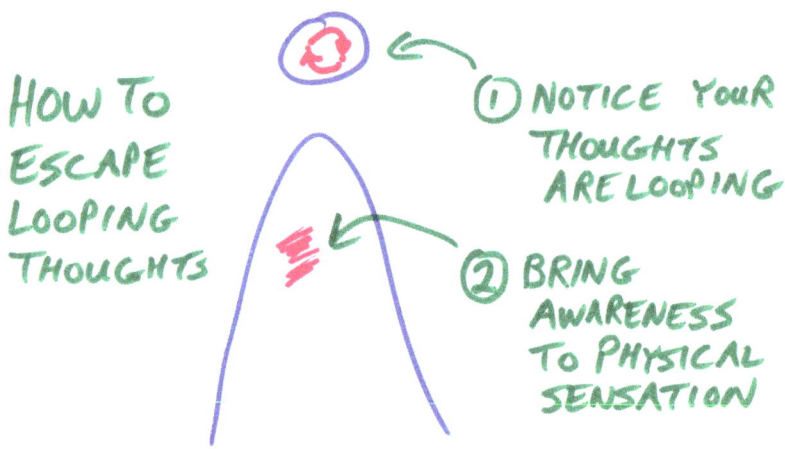

Diagram 9: Trap #1: Looping Thoughts

Escape Looping Thoughts
To escape Looping Thoughts, here is what to do:
1. Recognize your thoughts are looping.
2. **Choose to stop the looping thought.**
3. Go through the **Emotional Freedom Checklist** in Chapter 6 to orient to the physical sensations in your body that are caused by an emotional wound from the past.
4. Use the **Get Clear Technique** to resolve the charge.

Of course, the key here is to **notice that you are having looping thoughts.** Remember that as you notice or observe the patterns they begin to disrupt. The patterns begin to dissolve and heal. This might take some practice. It is important to let go of self-judgment. This happens to all of us. Choosing to look at the physical sensations sets you on the path for a healthier life.

TRAP #2:
Caught In A Story

The mind is a story-making machine.

*When there is a story,
there is an emotional wound.*

These stories come in many shapes and sizes:
- **Explanation:** Factually explaining why something is the way it is (especially when no one has asked).
- **Justification:** Creating a justification for why something is the way it is.
- **Blaming others:** Assigning blame for something.
- **Self-judgment:** "It's my fault." (Self-blame.)
- **Victim story:** "Poor me; everyone is out to get me."
- **Villain story:** "This person is responsible—they are the problem."

Let's go through an example so you get this.

Imagine you are meeting a friend for dinner and you show up late. Here are the stories you can tell about the situation:
- **Explanation:** "I left fifty minutes ago, so much traffic, I was stuck on the highway…"
- **Justification:** "It's not my fault. I left early enough."

- **Blaming others:** "The city should do a better job with infrastructure. And those construction companies don't seem to care about people needing to travel…traffic was really bad."
- **Self-judgment:** "Hey, sorry I am late. It is totally my fault. I should have left earlier."
- **Victim story:** "I am always the one getting stuck in traffic. I'm late for everything."
- **Villain story:** "Why did you even pick this location? You knew where I would be driving from!"

The emotional charges and wound for this example may be a family pattern and belief system stating that smart, responsible people are never late. The emotional wounding would have been created when you came late to a family dinner and you were scolded by your grandfather, a very judgmental man. The reaction from your grandfather hurt you, causing the original wounding and creating a series of trauma from this point forward.

All of these examples are evidence of confabulation. In other words, the mind creates a story to explain away a situation. The story doesn't even need to make sense or be true.

> *When you are in an emotional charge, your mind creates a story to avoid experiencing the charge. This is done to protect you from re-experiencing the pain of the emotional wound, since the mind does not know the difference between physical pain and psychological pain.*

Diagram 10: Trap #2: Caught In A Story

Escape The Story Trap
To release yourself from The Story trap, here is what to do:
1. Recognize that you are telling a story (see the list of how your mind tells stories and the examples above).
2. Go through the **Emotional Freedom Checklist** in Chapter 6 to orient to the physical sensations in your body that are caused by an emotional wound from the past.
3. Use the **Get Clear Technique** to resolve the charge.

It may take some time and effort to pay attention and admit that you are stuck in a story trap.

A common pattern is to create a story or an explanation for why something happened. On the surface, it's all very logical. Very rational. The real question to ask is: "Why am I thinking or saying this explanation? No one is asking it of me. I am simply making it up for myself."

At these moments, when the story stops and you look inward, you can experience the emotional charge that is causing you to create an explanation.

At this point you may say, "I really did my best," or, "there really was traffic." Remember we are creating our own reality, we are powerful beings. Just take a moment to be completely honest with yourself in the experience and ask yourself: *Is there a charge and is there an emotional wound?*

Sub-Trap: Let Go Of The "Why"
Another important sub-trap to notice is **the story of "Why."**

> *"Why is this emotional charge and the emotional wound here?"*

It is important to remember that this book is designed for you to bring awareness to the emotional charges and the emotional wounds. Once you have this awareness, it is important to then **let go of the story and go directly to the Get Clear Technique.** It is about releasing the charges and the wounds and letting go of the stories completely. The trap of the mind is subtle and we will gently remind you that all this information is for you to have healthier responses in all life's relationships and situations. This will lead to having a clear, effective, and easier life.

TRAP #3:
Arguing

Have you ever gotten into an argument? One where you really wanted someone else to agree with your point of view? A time where it got really heated?

Diagram 11: Trap #3: Arguing

When we are totally calm and emotionally clear we know that people have different perspectives. There is no need for someone to agree with our point of view. We might like that they agree with our point of view, yet we will be fine even if they don't agree with us. And further, we know intellectually that we can't make someone agree with us. They have to choose to agree of their own free will. And the most successful way to convince someone starts with listening to their perspective first. A deeper teaching here is to notice that you want to convince someone to agree with your point of view. Arguing can be abolished with letting go of your agenda, a need to be right, or have someone agree with your point of view.

We know that in highly productive environments, people respect each other and genuinely want to hear other perspectives. We are curious of what we might learn from others. We desire to make intelligent decisions based on shared wisdom and understanding. We know not to fall into the trap of cognitive bias and keep open to other ideas. And for most of this, it is far from our typical experience at work and in relationships. We become attached to our ideas. We want to be right. We think the other person is wrong. And we want to prove it to them. We want to look smart and have our idea acknowledged. Or we just want to talk and be heard, as our ideas are important or more important than others.

It has become easy to overlook these patterns of behavior. Everyone else functions in these patterns, as well; and it is easy to get swept up in the moment.

Exercise:
Exploring How Arguments Feel

It's easy to check this out for yourself. Just remember the last time you were in an argument. How did it feel in your body? Take a few moments to notice how it feels in your body when you are arguing with someone.

Escape The Arguing Trap
How to get out of the Arguing Trap? Here is what to do:
1. Recognize that you are arguing.
2. **Choose to stop arguing.**
3. Go through the **Emotional Freedom Checklist** in Chapter 6 to orient to the physical sensations in your body.
4. Use the **Get Clear Technique** to resolve the charge.

TRAP #4:
Complaining And Venting

If you are like most people, you have complained about someone or a situation that bothers you. What usually happens is that we feel frustrated and we start venting and complaining about the thing that is frustrating us. This is normal behavior in our society. And it is damaging to us and to others.

We are not referring to communicating with others to talk about a situation or to understand it so we can take effective action. What is explained here are those conversations where we are in a negative state and are talking in a negative way about a person or life situations. Some may call this gossiping or colluding with others. We have become habitual in our patterns of behavior where it is not obvious this is what is happening. There is an emotional wound that is triggered without an appropriate means to have a healthy response.

The behavior of complaining and venting has 2 components. The first is a form of releasing an emotional charge in an unhealthy way. It usually involves gossiping and colluding and trying to get others to be on your side and get their approval, to validate your point of view.

The second is that there is an energetic component to the negativity. This negative behavior is actually a virus, and infects the person receiving the complaint or listening to your venting. This is how we unconsciously spread negative energy, very quickly. Even a small comment about the "bad" weather spreads negative energy to the person you are speaking with. As a result it infects that person and their state becomes more negative. Spending a long time with negative people (1 negative person takes out 5 positive people) will create a negative environment where it becomes very difficult to have positive thoughts, feelings, or emotions.

When we are free and clear of negativity, we have a healthy way of responding to people and situations. We are truly only able to do this when we are free of emotional charges and emotional wounding. Having mastery over our behavior becomes important to not only our own physical and psychological health, but also to the health and well-being of those we relate to in our personal and professional relationships.

Exercise:
Exploring The Venting Trap

Take a moment to think of a time when you were complaining or venting about someone or a situation. What did it feel like in your body? What did the complaining accomplish for you? What is or was the payoff?

When we complain, we hang on to a negative energetic state. And even worse—we suck other people around us into the same place.

Escape The Complaining And Venting Trap
How to get out of the Complaining Trap? Here is what to do:
1. Recognize that you are complaining.
2. **Choose to stop complaining**.
3. Go through the **Emotional Freedom Checklist** in Chapter 6 to orient to the physical sensations in your body.
4. Use the **Get Clear Technique** to resolve the charge.

Summary Of Mind Traps
To Enhance Emotional Awareness

By now you may have noticed a theme in each of the traps: it starts with *noticing* a behavior that you do on a regular basis that does not serve you. In fact, you can identify your own favorite traps: it's any behavior that you do on a regular basis that does not serve you. Why would you act in a way that does not serve you? Only one reason: an emotional charge is impairing thinking.

Clear the charge, clear the thinking. It's that simple.

*Why would you act in a way that does not serve you?
Only one reason: an emotional charge
is impairing thinking.*

Now through Enhanced Emotional Awareness, you can have more success in life by noticing when automatic behaviors are taking you away from extraordinary results.

CHAPTER 9

Advanced Topics

IN THIS CHAPTER we will take you on a deeper tour of your inner world of emotions. The additional clarity of how your emotions work will support your ability to notice when you are stuck in them so you can recover. In addition to learning new models, you will also continue to have an inner exploration through a series of exercises.

Doorways For Healing

Now that you have an awareness of emotional charges, consider the following question:

**How many times a day do you have
an emotional charge come up?**

Society has conditioned us not to notice our emotional state. One might think that days might go by without an emotional charge coming up. In practice, once you start to look—to *really* look—you will see that emotional charges come up hundreds of times a day. A little frustration here, a little disappointment there. And if we dig into them we find how powerful the charges are, and how much they impact our ability to flow with life and others.

We call these **doorways for healing.** Each charge is an emotional wound. Each disruption in life becomes a chance to heal an emotional wound. To become more whole. More adaptable. More able to flow with life's waves.

You can gain the ability to become more resourceful in any situation so you can pick the best action available to get more of what you want.

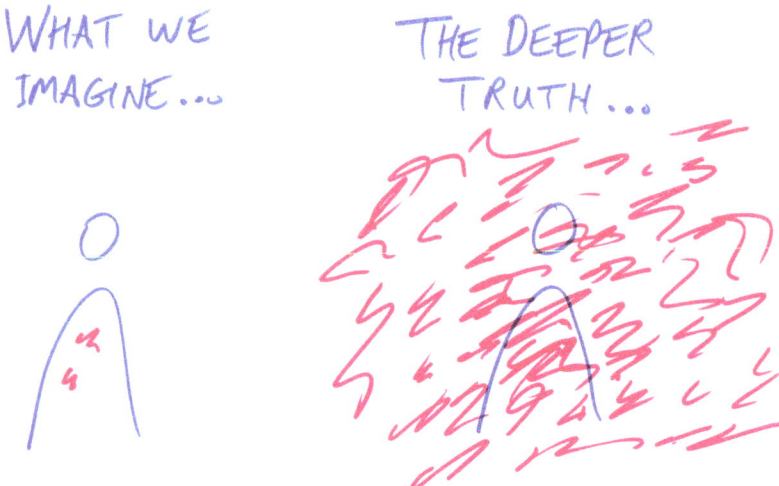

Diagram 12: Doorways For Healing

Diagram 14 shows Michael's understanding and growing awareness of his emotional landscape. Every time a charge came up, he rapidly went through the Emotional Freedom Checklist to orient to what was happening and then decide what to do about it. Sometimes it was just taking a few deep breaths because that was all that was possible in the situation. Sometimes it was taking a time out to use the Get Clear Technique. For a few months, Michael used this technique many times a day. This is a key part of his daily practice to the point where it is almost automatic and second nature.

Exercise:
Handling Multiple Emotional Charges

By now you may have noticed that sometimes you experience more than one physical sensation in your body. As each physical sensation is related to an emotional charge, it means that there is more than one charge coming up at the same time. It is normal for a single situation to activate multiple interconnected neural networks that all fire and bring up a set of self-supporting emotional charges and wounds. Working through this is very possible, it just takes a little more time and care.

Here is some guidance for working through this:
1. **Identify all the charges that have physical sensations.**
2. **Acknowledge them and check the intensity (1…10).**
3. **Identify the most intense charge.**
4. **Apply the techniques in this book on *just the one* most intense charge.**
5. **Once the intensity lowers, focus on the next most intense charge.**
6. **Repeat this process moving from charge to charge.**

Exercise:
Accelerate Your Growth At The Movies

Most of us understand a movie as a source of entertainment and sometimes even an escape from life. Movies are also a powerful tool for self-introspection and growth.

As you already know, daily life provides many opportunities to see emotional charges and they are doorways for healing. By simply pausing and noticing what is happening in your emotional landscape and then applying the techniques you learned, your inner world will repattern quickly.

Why stop there? You can use watching movies as a way to elicit strong emotional reactions. While watching a movie, if you hit a charge (a strong emotional reaction), pause the movie and apply the techniques of the Emotional Freedom System.

In this way, you can undertake preventive maintenance on your emotional system. You will clear emotional charges and wounds without having to wait for a life situation to appear. Using movies will accelerate your growth. It also gives you a safe environment in which to grow since you are in full control.

For The Curious:
A Deeper Understanding Of Emotional Wounds

Recall your results from the exercise in Chapter 3: When Life Hits Us, when you noticed your strong emotional reactions or charges from 3 different situations. You noticed your thoughts and feelings, you felt physical sensations in your body, and you saw how you reacted to a situation. But what about the original situation itself that caused these charges?

Let's take a closer look at Table 4 from Chapter 4.

TIME 0 →	TIME 1 →	TIME 2 →	TIME 3 →	TIME 4 → ... etc.
ORIGINAL EMOTIONAL WOUND CREATION	Emotional Charge	Emotional Charge	Emotional Charge	Emotional Charge

Recap Of Table 4: Emotional Wound Time-Lapse

Emotional charges, which occur at Time 1, Time 2, Time 3, Time 4, etc., are only symptoms of the root cause. TIME 0 — the emotional wound itself, can be otherwise known as the "original" source of your recurring experiences.

*The root cause is the actual trauma or
life event that created the emotional wound.*

The emotional wound, without being healed, continues to cause blocks and obstacles in your life.

Recall that *an emotional wound is an unprocessed emotion from the past that lives within the body.* The unprocessed emotional wound is re-experienced through charges and the charges are causing damage in life. By going through this process, you are coming to the root cause of the unprocessed emotions stored within your body. Healing your emotional wounds removes the blockages that prevent you from getting extraordinary results and unlocking high performance.

Once you become aware of your "original" wound at TIME 0, you will see charges from an emotional wound arising frequently throughout your day. Those same wounds will get re-experienced in your life over and over again. This is normal.

Generally the test is: if you remembered something from less than age 6 then you can assume that it is definitely something real. If something happened when you were a teenager or older, it is usually an earlier precipitated event that you don't have conscious access to.

A Neuro-Linguistic Programming practitioner might say, "When is the first time you experienced this event? Before, during, or after your birth?" Other practitioners suggest traumas originate from inside the womb, when you are really young, or even from a past life.

Science tells us that important neurological development occurs while we are still a fetus. We can even presuppose that traumas can happen when the neurological system is first forming, or even when the very first cells are being developed as the neurological system forms patterns based on what the mother was experiencing while pregnant.

There is really no way to know when your original wound happened, and it doesn't even really matter. What happens when the wound is created is not really important.

Using the Get Clear Technique can be applied to the root cause, as well as the emotional charges, as long as you can identify the physical or bodily sensations that come when you identify the root cause of the emotional wound.

An emotional wound is only something that can be experienced in the body. The way that you can explain what happened is just the mind's way of encoding information. The mind will invent all kinds of different stories in order to understand the emotional wound. It does not matter if what you have experienced is literally true.

Holistic View Of Emotions

Up until now, the focus here has been on individual emotions arising and how we might increase our awareness of them to get more of the life we want. What is shared in this section is a guide for advanced practitioners to observe the bigger picture of what is happening inside our beings. As you practice the Emotional Freedom System, you will increase your awareness of what is happening and may discover what we share here.

Michael first noticed his internal conflict in his early 20s when he was working on his master's thesis in Artificial Intelligence. While working out how to create a controller program for soccer playing robots, Michael closed his eyes and observed his inner reality. He witnessed different emotions competing for control. Through this he created a control program called Reactive Deliberation where parts of the program would compete internally for control of the robot's actions.

Emotions In Conflict

Have you seen the movie *Inside Out*? We highly recommend that you watch it. Why? First of all, it's funny. You will also get to re-experience emotional wounds. More importantly, it will help you understand the contents of this section much better.

In the movie, different emotions are in conflict for who gets to control the thoughts and behavior of the protagonist. This is not far from the truth. Real life is similar to the movie. In the movie, individual emotions (Joy, Sadness, Anger, Fear, Disgust) compete for control. In real life, it is the emotional charges that arise from emotional wounds that are competing for control.

When you observe your inner reality, you may notice that different emotional wounds are active and are pulling toward different actions. **Here's a diagram to illustrate this:**

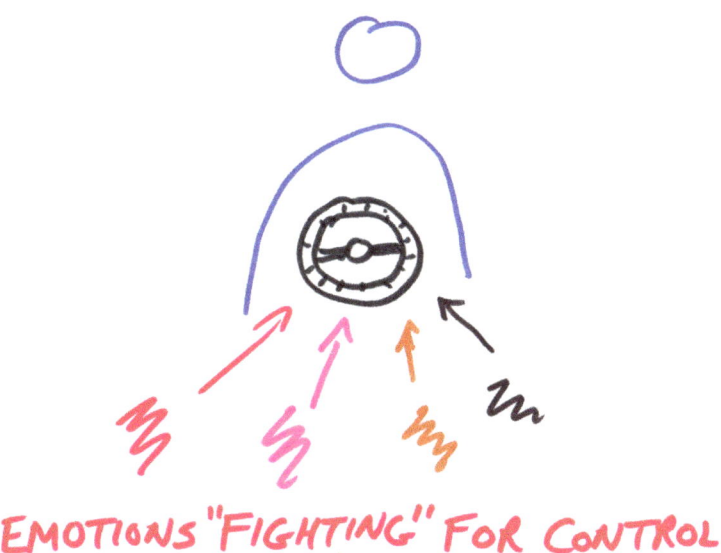

Diagram 13: Emotions Fighting For Control

Any given situation in the world will activate not one, but multiple patterns. Each one will come with an emotional wound. The adaptive behavior for each wound will want a different action. With that comes a cluster of desired behaviors that may be in conflict with one another; like in the movie, the emotional wounds are fighting with each other to grab the steering wheel and take control. If you want to imagine the fictional emotional characters from the movie, you might think of emotional wounds as what is motivating each of them to take action. And you will need a lot more characters than the 5 in the movie since we carry within us hundreds of emotional wounds.

Exercise:
Inner Investigation Of Emotions In Conflict

1. Identify a situation where you found yourself in conflict.
2. Revisit the situation with your imagination so it feels like it is happening now.
3. Notice that multiple distinct physical sensations are present.
4. Notice that the sensations "want" different things in the situation.

That is how we live: in constant internal struggle. So much energy is wasted on this internal conflict. It's draining energy and life. Now that the larger picture is clear, the value of practicing the Emotional Freedom System becomes even clearer: it is a path toward inner freedom from conflict.

Emotions And Personality Patterns

We're now going to present another model that is helpful for understanding what is happening in your inner world. It is introduced to support your growing awareness of your inner state.

As you have learned and discovered through the previous exercises and various examples, our nervous system makes adaptations to our inner world to protect us. When a belief is formed and becomes deeply ingrained with your personality, a behavior pattern is created to energetically hold the emotional wound. Therefore, we can have multiple personality patterns as each emotional wound comes with its own belief system and a set of behaviors. These patterns allow us to react automatically to situations. This is useful for survival, but not for living the life we want.

Some examples of personality patterns are:
- **Perfectionist:** Wanting everything to be perfect/correct/best.
- **Superior:** Wanting to be better than everyone else; jealous of other people's success.
- **Distancing:** Wanting to protect the self by disconnecting from others and not speaking.
- **Accomplishment:** Only caring about getting things done and not about people.
- **Recognition:** Wanting to be seen, recognized, and admired.
- **Slacker:** Avoiding or procrastinating; not wanting responsibility.

Everyone has personality patterns. Everyone has a personality. There is nothing wrong with it. This is a natural process.

Personality patterns are the mechanism that emotions use to take control of our behavior.

Let's look at how this plays out in life.

Diagram 14: Emotions Fuel Personality

In the previous section you looked at how emotional wounds are pulling you in different directions. When you look deeper into how they move you toward action, you will notice that emotional wounds activate a personality pattern. This is depicted in Diagram 14 as a small inner you. Multiple emotional wounds will fuel a given personality pattern.

It feels like parts of you are pulling in different directions. Fighting for control. Coming back to the movie *Inside Out* that was mentioned earlier, it's not really the emotions that are fighting for control; it's the personality patterns. One is wasting energy in conflict.

Everyone has personality patterns that are not supporting them in living the life they want. You may have believed that is just how you are and there is nothing you can do about it. Until now.

Have you ever noticed how your personality changes from one situation to another? How you "show up" is based on the environment: who you are with and what is happening. The way you behave with your family is different than how you behave with your friends and how you "show up" at work. The personality you exhibit at work is different from the one with friends or family.

For every situation there is a different personality pattern showing up. Depending on the situation and person you are relating to, various triggers can activate various wounds. The brain is constantly trying to match present experiences with past experiences. Our behavior is complicated because we are a bunch of personalities and patterns created from the past expressing in the present.

Now that you can see emotional wounds are the fuel for unresourceful behavior, you can use the Emotional Freedom System to rewire your behavior so you can achieve more success in your life.

Exercise:
Inventory Of Personality Patterns

1. **Personal reflection:** Get in nature or put on some relaxing music and take note of your personality patterns. Take out a blank sheet of paper or start journaling in your notebook. See how many patterns you can identify that govern your behavior. Remind yourself that this is normal — we all have patterns — you may notice many patterns.
2. **Ask your friends and family:** Ask your loved ones what the main features of your personality are. Of course, it will help if you explain to them why you are doing this and give them a hint as to what you are looking for.

Exercise:
Investigation Of Conflicting Personality Parts

1. Identify a situation where you found yourself in conflict.
2. Revisit the situation with your imagination so it feels like it is happening now.
3. Notice what personality patterns are active.
4. Notice what the personality patterns "want" you to do in the situation.
5. Notice that there is an emotional charge or physical sensation for each one.

Application

Now that you have discovered the secret inner workings of your reality, what do you do about it?

The secret ingredient of the Emotional Freedom System is **awareness**. Now that you are aware of the inner workings of your reality, it becomes much easier to spot when you are reacting from an emotional wound.

Here is what to do:
1. Notice you are in **conflict**.
2. Notice the parts that are pulling you in different directions.
3. For each part, apply the **Emotional Freedom System, stop, and use the Get Clear Technique.**

Bottom line: notice you are in conflict
and it's time to *Get Clear.*

Operating From Your True Self

What happens when you are clear inside? What is it like when you are no longer in internal conflict? The diagram below illustrates this state:

Diagram 15: When Emotions Are Quiet

When all the emotional conflict stops, you are left in a state of inner peace. An inner quiet. From this peace we gain the clarity we need to be effective. High performance requires clarity. When one is clear it becomes easy to step into a state of flow, where high performance activates success at all levels of life, relationships, career, purpose and health. A place where you can create a life in exactly the way you want to live. One might call this place your true self or your highest self. World wisdom traditions call this enlightenment.

Your awakened awareness recognizes this as your new goal. Each and every step in that direction will help you get even more extraordinary results. Enjoy the journey.

CHAPTER 10

Continue The Journey

Where's The Science?

SCIENCE IS HERE to help us understand our world. But how can we prove something as intangible, unique, and personal like emotions?

Since emotions are based on our inner experiences, we need to create our own way to examine and work with them. If you have taken the time to apply the exercises then you will have experimentally proven the models in this book. Why? You have taken observations. You have tested hypotheses to see how they fit your inner reality. You have tested and likely revised your beliefs about how emotions work.

Congratulations! You are an experimental scientist!

The book is not just science, it's Applied Science since you can get practical results from its application. For example, you might have noticed benefits from applying the Emotional Freedom System.

Let's Check In On Your Understanding

After taking the time to apply the information, it's time to check to see how valuable this book has been for you. Let's start by checking in with the question posed in Chapter 2:

Exercise:
How Well Do You Understand How Your Emotions Work?

1 2 3 4 5 6 7 8 9 10

(Circle your best answer as quickly as possible. Your first instinct is the most accurate.)

10: You are 100% clear about how emotions work. You understand exactly where they come from. You know how they relate to your thoughts. You are absolutely certain about how they work.

1: You don't understand. It could be that examining your belief system seems quite confusing. Or you may understand how you think about emotions, but have no idea if you are right.

Briefly check your results from the Chapter 2 Exercise: How Well Do You Understand How Your Emotions Work? Ideally your score went up and you now have a better understanding of your emotions. And, congratulations! This work is not for the faint of heart; no matter what your score is, congratulate yourself for the willingness to explore your inner world.

Yet, that's not what this book is really about. It is about being more effective in your life. It's about reducing the damage caused by out of control emotions and bringing us back to a calm, resourced place so we can be successful and enjoy life. Let's check in with where you are on these questions:

I am doing a better job noticing my emotions
Strongly Disagree   Disagree   Neutral   Agree   Strongly Agree

I am applying the Emotional Freedom System daily
Strongly Disagree   Disagree   Neutral   Agree   Strongly Agree

I am feeling better on a day-to-day basis than I did before I learned this information

Strongly Disagree   Disagree   Neutral   Agree   Strongly Agree

My relationships with others have improved

Strongly Disagree   Disagree   Neutral   Agree   Strongly Agree

We hope you have noticed an improvement in your life. That is why we wrote the book: to help you live a more full and happy existence. In doing this work of taking ownership of your inner experience and your life, you contribute to making the world a better place. Through this inner work you can function at your fullest potential to manifest an extraordinary life.

Continuing Your Journey

The exercises in *Emotional Science* are a foundation for your emotional healing work. The reality is that emotional development never truly ends. As you continue your own emotional healing, you may eventually need access to further resources to continue developing your practice.

Audio Version Of The Get Clear Technique

You can download the guided Get Clear Technique from the website **www.emotionalscience.com/download**. Note: if downloaded the exercises earlier, you already have access to this.

Live Courses

We are conducting in-person workshops that will take you deeper into these teachings. Please go to **www.emotionalscience.com** for upcoming live events.

Stay Connected
We encourage you to sign up for our mailing list so that we can support your learning journey with useful tips and any upcoming in-person training at: **www.emotionalscience.com.**

Work With Us
We know that it can be a challenge to work through this on your own. If you are interested in getting help from our team of coaching professionals, please contact us at: **info@emotionalscience.com.**

Conscious Leadership For High Performance
Michael and Audree are world experts in developing the consciousness of leaders to create high-performance organizations. If you are interested in learning more, please visit their website: **www.agilitrix.com.**

Closing

We would like to thank you for your courage and your willingness to explore the deepest regions of your being, to go beyond the constructs of your mind, and to smooth out the places where emotions have become the obstacles that stop you from creating a higher quality of life.

It is easy to blame others and continue to numb out reality. It has been easy for humanity to overlook the possibility of creating life that is effortless, healthy, and abundant.

We applaud your willingness to take action, especially when this action is uncomfortable and even strange at first. We are humbled to be in service to this work. We are blessed to have taken ourselves through these practices to know the truth of our behaviors and to learn a new way of showing up in life, in our relationships, and the creation of our reality. Thank you for investing your time and energy to find the same results with this work.

*May the strength of your conviction
and the willingness to become clear and whole
be met with an overflow of Grace...
May an effortless inner peace arise within
to create an extraordinary life for yourself
and for those whose you touch.*

*In Peace,
Audree Tara and Michael K Sahota*

References

Prologue — Michael

1. Brown, Brené. *I Thought It Was Just Me: Women Reclaiming Power and Courage in a Culture of Shame.* New York: Gotham Books, A Division of Penguin Group (USA) Inc., 2007.

2. McGonigal, Jane, and Keith Wakeman. "Super Better." SuperBetter, LLC. 2018. www.superbetter.com.

Chapter 4

1. "What Are The Seven Emotions?" Shen-Nong Ltd. 2006. www.shen-nong.com/eng/principles/sevenemotions.html.

2. Maté, Gabor. "Compassionate Inquiry." Seminar, Toronto, ON, Canada, November 3–4, 2016.

Chapter 5

1. Frankl, Viktor E. *Man's Search for Meaning.* Boston: Beacon Press, 2006; first published in German under the title *Ein Psycholog erlebt das Konzentrationslager.* Original English title was *From Death-Camp to Existentialism,* 1946.

Further Reading

Barrett, Lisa Feldman. *How Emotions Are Made: The Secret Life of the Brain.* New York: Houghton Mifflin Harcourt, 2017.

Brach, Tara. *Radical Acceptance: Embracing Your Life With the Heart of a Buddha.* New York: Bantam Books, 2003.

Maté, Gabor. *When The Body Says No: Understanding the Stress-Disease Connection.* New York: Random House, 2011.

Miller, Alice. *Prisoners Of Childhood: The Drama of the Gifted Child and the Search for the True Self.* New York, First Basic Books edition: 1981; reissued 1996. Originally published in German under the title *Das Drama des begabten Kindes*, 1979.

Tolle, Eckhart. *The Power of Now.* Novato, California and Vancouver, B.C., Canada: Namaste Publishing and New World Library, 2004.

Van Der Kolk, Bessel. *The Body Keeps the Score: Brain, Mind, and Body in the Healing of Trauma.* New York: Penguin Books, 2014.